Lighting the Global Lantern

A Teacher's Guide to Writing Haiku and Related Literary Forms

Lighting the Global Lantern

A Teacher's Guide to Writing Haiku and Related Literary Forms

Terry Ann Carter

WINTERGREEN STUDIOS PRESS
Township of South Frontenac
Ontario, Canada

Wintergreen Studios Press
P.O. Box 75, Yarker, ON, Canada K0K 3N0

"The Hilltop Temple" by Matsuo Bashō (translated by Dorothy Britton) appears in *A Haiku Journey/Narrow Road to a Far Province*, Kodansha International Ltd., 1974; "Baseball Season" by Cor van den Heuvel, *A Boy's Seasons: Haibun Memoirs*, Single Island Press, 2010; "The Haiku Roadshow" by LeRoy Gorman, first appeared as a presentation to the Haiku Canada conference, McGill University, 2010; "Literary Inspiration for Writing Haiku" by Penny Harter; "Haiku for the ESL Students" by Raffael de Gruttola, adapted from the foreword to the *Anthology for the Massachusetts Association for Bilingual Association*, 1990; "31 October: Siem Reap" by John Brandi, *Water Shining Beyond the Fields*, Tres Chicas Books, 2006; "Inspiration for Remembrance: Haiku of War and Peace" by Rick Black, adapted from the preface to *Peace and War: A Collection of Haiku from Israel*, Turtle Light Press, 2007; "Consonance as the Genesis of Humour in Haiku" and "Haiku and Beyond: The Haiku Slam and More" by Randy Brooks; "The Universe in Three Lines: Exploring New Worlds with Speculative Haiku" by Deborah Kolodji, first appeared in *Haiku Canada Review*; "Youth Participation: The International Haiku Conference" by Rich Schnell; "Haiku and Visual Art" by Pamela Miller Ness used with permission of the author, first appeared as a presentation for the Haiku North America Conference, Boston, 2001; "Books, Books, and More" by Terry Ann Carter, first appeared, in an earlier version, as a presentation for the Learning Through the Arts Conference, Ottawa, 2007; "2010 Haiku Invitational Winners: A Judge's Perspective" by Michael Dylan Welch, first appeared on http://www.vcbf.com; "Why Haiku?" by Sherry Zhou; "The Improper Use of Semicolons" by Roberta Beary, *Modern Haiku*, 39:3 (Pushcart Prize nomination); *White Lies*, Red Moon Press, 2008; "bar fly" by Roberta Beary, *Contemporary Haibun Online* June 2005, 1:1; "Haibun: Union of Prose and Poetry" by John Dunphy published in *cho* with permission of the author, originally published by the *Saint Louis Dispatch Online*, March 21, 2009; "My longing for you" by Ono no Komachi; "No different, really" by Lady Izumi Shikibu; "I've this memory" by Michael McClintock; "her china cup" by Lois Harvey; "I know" by Owen Bullock, *Modern English Tanka*, 3:3, 2009; "I'm showing off again" by Owen Bullock, *Atlas Poetica*, 3, 2009; "spin the bottle," "peer pressured," and "outside the church" by Pamela Babusci; "benched" by Barry George, *Modern English*

Tanka, 2:3; "for me" by Barry George, Gusts, 9: Spring/Summer 09; "4 am" and "crowds exit" by Helen Buckingham, *Modern English Tanka*, 3:2, 2008; "Notes on Form, Techniques, and Subject Matter in Modern English Tanka," adapted from Michael McClintock, *The Tanka Anthology*, Red Moon Press, 2003 edited by Michael McClintock, Pamela Miller Ness, and Jim Kacian; "dead cat..." by Michael McClintock; "lovers" by George Swede; "I cover the goldfish bowl" by Emiko Miyashita, *Haiku of America Society Anthology*, 2006; "first date" by Michael Dylan Welch; "gelled hair" by Angela Leuck; "this cold morning" by Michael McClintock; "sun sets" by George Swede; "endless scales" by Dorothy Howard in *Haiku, Anthologie Canadienne/Canadian Anthology*, 1985; "looking for something" by Ce Rosenow, *Pacific*, Mountain Gate Press, 2009; "end of the story" by Francine Banwarth, *Frogpond*, 30:2; "liking the same music" by John Stevenson, *Upstate Dim Sum*, 2008/1; "he gives me" by Keri Haas, Virgilio contest finalist, 1990; "beautiful girl" by Matt Richards, Virgilio contest finalist, 1992; "inside the box" by Noelle Egan, Virgilio contest finalist, 1993; "first date" by Scott Splinter, Virgilio contest finalist, 1996; "signs of spring" by Dani DeCaro, Virgilio contest finalist, 1998; "at the movie" by Paula Faber, Virgilio contest finalist, 1999; "harvest moon" by Kate Bosek-Sills, Virgilio contest finalist, 2005; "light footsteps" by Desire Giddens, Virgilio contest finalist, 2008; "spring" by Marco Fraticelli, *Carpe Diem*, 2007; "barbeque by the ocean" by Marco Fraticelli, *Voyeur Guernica Editions*, 1992; "summer afternoon..." by Stanford M. Forrester, *Asahi Shimbun/ International Tribune* (Japan); "in the meadow" by Penny Harter, is a verse from a solo renga "Brushing Grey Hair," *In the Broken Curve*, Burnt Lake Press, 1984; "Feb. 15" by Grant D. Savage; all other poems by Grant D. Savage from *Their White With Them*, Bondi Studios, 2007; "December Morning" by Lenard D. Moore and Fay Aoyagi, *Haiku Canada Review*.

Canadian Cataloguing in Publication Data
Lighting the Global Lantern: A Teacher's Guide to Writing Haiku and Related Literary Forms

ISBN-10: 098654731X EAN-13: 978-0-9865473-1-7
Carter, Terry Ann, 1946—

I.   Title.

Legal Deposit—Library and Archives Canada 2011

Book and cover design by R. Upitis.
Cover photo by T. A. Carter, in Kuala Lumpur, Malaysia.
Author photo by Claudia Coutu Radmore.

For Dylan and Barrett

Other books by Terry Ann Carter

Waiting for Julia (1999)

such green (2005)

Transplanted (2006)

Road Trip: More Latte Than Turquoise on the Road from Ottawa to Santa Fe (2008)

Crossing Yangstze (2008)

A Crazy Man Thinks He's Ernest in Paris (2010)

A Monk's Fine Robes: Haiku from Cambodia (2011)

Now You Know I Can Change My Mind (2011)

To the village lights
I add my own lantern:
spring festival

     Yoshiko Yoshino, Japan

first day of spring
the skateboarder
almost flying

     Terry Ann Carter, Canada

The way we see the world shapes the way we treat it.

David Suzuki, Canadian environmentalist,
educator, author

Haiku is a literary art equipped with antennas that can send loving messages from the whole of creation on Earth — plains and mountains, rivers, lakes, and oceans, and plants and animals, including humankind. If people in the entire world became haiku-minded and nurtured Mother Nature, then it might be possible to sustain the life on our planet for the benefit of future generations.

Yoshiko Yoshino, Japanese haiku poet

Haiku is an awakening of the spirit — away from technocratic rationality, away from the sophistication, attention seeking and glitter. Back to basics. Our time is in need of simplicity.

Herman Van Rompuy,
European Union President, haiku poet

There are day to day miracles happening outside the classroom. Get kids into wild areas where Nature does the teaching, affecting students in ways that stick with them for the rest of their lives.

Karsten Heurer, explorer, wildlife biologist,
author

Table of Contents

Preface

Lighting the Global Lantern is a writing guide for teachers and students in secondary and post-secondary schools, and for anyone with a teen-aged spirit who wants to learn more about the aha! poetry of our time.

By writing haiku about the self first, teens may journey from self, to community, through nature, to the cosmos. Teachers and students alike may begin to look at nature in a compassionate way, and understand the deep cycles of themselves embedded in a universal knowledge of empathy and wisdom.

Lighting the Global Lantern will introduce teachers and students to new perspectives on writing haiku, haibun (prose and haiku combined), tanka (a five lined poetry with more emotional impact), linked haiku, and haiga (image and haiku combined). Each chapter includes traditional examples of the genre as well as contemporary versions. Writing suggestions, references, and websites for those who want to pursue these subjects in more detail are also included. Some of the content of these sites will give histories and biographies concerning the origins of haiku and related literary forms, others will give up-to-the-minute blogging notes from haiku poets living in cities across North America. Articles on various topics: Haiku and Literature, War and Peace, Haiku and Visual Art, Haiku and Comics, Finding Inspiration, Haiku and the ESL teacher, plus more, are included to provide up to date information from world class haiku poets and educators.

With the current emphasis on eco-literacy, environmental studies, sustainability, and "greening the curriculum," learning how to write haiku might become the first step to a reconciliation with nature that could foster compassion and survival.

I would like to thank haiku poet friends from around the world who helped with the itinerary of this book. Foremost, my collaborator from the start, Angela Leuck in Montréal, Québec. Special thanks to haiku poets Philomene Kocher (Ontario) and Barry George (Pennsylvania) who helped with early versions of the text. For my Japanese haiku poet and friend Emiko Miyashita, who wrote during the bleak hours of Japan's recent earthquake, a deep bow of gratitude, and to Sanford Goldstein, mentor, teacher to hundreds—a special acknowledgement for your correspondence from Japan during this terrible time. Your tanka spirit has inspired many poets throughout the haiku world and I am privileged to include your story. Penny Harter (New Jersey) and Raffael de Gruttola (Massachusetts) contributed the first of many articles over two years ago. Garry Gay (California), Jim Kacian (Virginia), Amelia Fielden, (Australia), Dr. Randy Brooks (Illinois), Dr. Rich Schnell (New York), Michael McClintock (California), and robert d. wilson (Philippines) also sent materials. To Pamela Miller Ness, Michael Dylan Welch, Cor van den Heuvel, John Dunphy, Jeff Winke, Jessica Tremblay,

John Brandi, Grant Savage: thank you for inspirational words and encouragement. For exquisite seasonal "haiku photographs" I would like to thank Paul Benoit, and for charming pen and ink line drawings, a thanks to Matt Cipov. These illustrations greatly enhance the haiga chapter which also includes beautiful traditional haiga by Rebecca Lyn Cragg and collaborators, plus exciting contemporary haiga by Naia.

I would like to thank Tony Virgilio for permission to reprint a number of Virgilio contest finalists and for important information concerning the international nature of the Nicholas A. Virgilio Memorial Haiku Competition for Grades 7 through 12.

My thanks, also, to Kathy Bacile, English teacher at Immaculata High School, Ottawa, and Dorothy Mahoney, East Essex High School, Windsor, Ontario, where I gave haiku and tanka workshops. These teachers provided informed, creative classrooms, and valuable feedback. Thanks also to teacher-librarian Urszula Gesikowska at Holy Trinity High School in Kanata, Ontario, where I participated, for the past five years, in haiku workshops as part of her April is Poetry Month. Thanks also to Denise Shannon at St. Paul's High School, Ottawa, and Jennifer Simpson, English Department Head at Mother Teresa High School, Ottawa, for inviting me to give poetry workshops and readings at their schools.

Without the dedication of Wintergreen Studios Press and the unimaginable stamina and enthusiasm for this project from Dr. Rena Upitis, *Lighting the Global Lantern* would still be in darkness. My appreciation and gratitude are boundless.

Terry Ann Carter
Ottawa, Ontario
2011

Why Haiku?

Haiku is more than a form of poetry; it is a way to read the text of the world by responding to nature, including our human nature. When David Suzuki challenges us to see the world as environmentalists, he invites a change in our attitudes. Haiku is in a unique position not only in its function as a poetic form in the language arts curriculum, but also in its potential to teach students about the connections between themselves and their environment. In a world that is becoming more and more complex with technological advances and ecological changes, helping students to build this awareness is more important than ever. Haiku poet Yoshiko Yoshino reminds us that being "haiku-minded" might help to foster attitudes of conservation and compassion for our planet. After presenting more than a hundred haiku workshops over the past two decades, I have come to the belief that students, as well as teachers, need to balance their busy lives with moments of introspection, with moments of aha! beauty, with dimensions of art-making that give sustainable purpose and commitment to creative activity.

Ministries of Education have this to say...

The following quotes from Canadian Curriculum Guidelines give us some ideas about student expectations.

> By the end of Grade 12, students will acquire knowledge, skills, and perspectives that foster understanding of their fundamental connections to each other, to the world around them, and to all living things. (*Acting Today, Shaping Tomorrow: A Policy Framework for Environmental Education in Ontario Schools*, Ontario Ministry of Education, 2009, p. 11)

> Environmental education should enable the students to: ... appreciate the resilience, fragility, and beauty of nature and develop respect for the place and function of all living things in the overall planetary ecosystem. (*Acting Today, Shaping Tomorrow: A Policy Framework for Environmental Education in Ontario Schools*, Ontario Ministry of Education, 2009, p. 27)

> Students should be provided with opportunities to develop an aesthetic appreciation of the environment. (*Environmental Education/Sustainable Societies*, British Columbia Ministry of Education, 1994)

As well as fostering positive attitudes, haiku and its related forms can be used to meet the requirements of Language Arts and English curricula: writing, reading and responding to literature, orality, and media literacy/ representation. The related forms extend haiku into longer prose pieces and visual imagery.

Educators have this to say

In 1915, in his seminal work *Schools of Tomorrow*, the American educator and philosopher John Dewey, wrote of the need for children to experience their environment—the need to appreciate the world of nature that surrounds them. Almost one hundred years later, his vision is still relevant, his words preceding the voices of environmentalists around the world.

Educator and poet Victoria Gaylie (2008) invited her urban, middle-school students to write poetry outdoors as a way of teaching ecoliteracy. Haiku was one of the forms she included. Her study showed "how nurturing a quiet, alert, poetic awareness toward the earth, provides a predisposition that permits ecoliterate knowledge to emerge in our students" (p. 13).

Arts educator Elliot Eisner (2002) describes work in the arts as a way to develop "a disposition to tolerate ambiguity, to explore what is uncertain…[and] such a disposition is at the root of the development of individual autonomy" (p. 10). In her graduate research, where she explored haiku with elderly men and women suffering from dementia, Philomene Kocher (2008) advocates that: "metaphorical understanding that allows room for ambiguity and uncertainty may help to build essential skills not only for future learning, but for navigating the complexities of life that follow graduation."

Haiku is a path for navigating those complexities.

Haiku

Part 1: Definition of haiku

A haiku is a short poem that uses imagistic language to convey the essence of an experience. It is what is happening "now." In Japanese, haiku consists of 17 *morae* (or *on*) "sound beats" written on one line. English language haiku are written on three lines or less, and are usually less than 17 syllables. These three lines are composed by juxtaposing two images together.

A haiku attempts to capture that aha! moment. It's a moment that you don't want to forget.

The moment, not the syllables, is what matters most.

Part 2: Examples of traditional Japanese haiku

each time the wind blows
the butterfly finds a new home
on the willow

Bashō

lingering
in every pool of water
spring sunlight

Issa

cold moon —
three stalks of bamboo
among the withered trees

Buson

snow
falls on snow —
silence

Santoka

moon flowers!
when a woman's skin
is revealed

Chiyo-ni

woman's desire
deeply rooted —
the wild violets

Chiyo-ni

Part 3: Examples of contemporary haiku

spring
melting
us

Marco Fraticelli

dead cat …
open mouthed
to the pouring rain

Michael McClintock

I cover the goldfish bowl
with a hotel shower cap
fish in love

Emiko Miyashita

divorce
nobody
wants the dog

Ruth Holzer

a face
in the darkness
cellphone glow

Melanie Noll

lovers
exchanging
bacteria

George Swede

barbeque by the ocean
the pork chops
shaped like Africa

Marco Fraticelli

first date
letting her
put snow down my neck

Michael Dylan Welch

sunfish
and origami rabbits
my nephew's phone call

Philomene Kocher

snow on black hoodies
the boys scarf back
lunch

Pearl Pirie

liking the same music
we hope the rest
will be easy

John Stevenson

end of the story
  I'll miss
the characters

Francine Banwarth

longing for something—
an unknown seabird
soars out of sight

Ce Rosenow

Student Haiku

The Nicholas A. Virgilio Memorial Haiku Competition for Grades 7 through 12 was founded in 1990 by the Sacred Heart Church in Camden, New Jersey. It is sponsored and administered by the Nick Virgilio Haiku Association in memory of Nicholas A. Virgilio, a charter member of the Haiku Society of America, who died in 1989.

The Haiku Society of America co-sponsors this international contest. For more information visit http://www. hsa. org. Here are some haiku by Virgilio contest finalists.

he gives me
roses
and their thorns

Keri Haas

beautiful girl
I turn my head and run
the red light

Matt Richards

strep throat
she kisses him
anyway

Heidi Streit

first date
her dog
likes me

Scott Splinter

signs of spring:
tanktop revealing
her butterfly tattoo

Dani DeCaro

at the movie
their hands meet . . .
in buttered popcorn

Paula Faber

light footsteps
across the snow
his alcohol breath

Desire Giddens

Part 4: How to write haiku

A haiku lets you express yourself in ways you never thought possible.

Most poets don't use capital letters at the beginning of a line of haiku.

Haiku do not rhyme.

Show, don't tell.

A haiku is similar to a photograph, for it "freezes" a moment, yet there is a difference.

Marco Fraticelli is a haiku poet living in Montréal. In the poet's own words, "The Kodak moment or photographic moment shows us what we already know or, ahhhhhhhhhhhhhhhh isn't that cute—the baby with his hands in the cake. The haiku moment makes us think about something that we've seen in a way we've never thought about before, a kind of epiphany, an aha! moment."

The language of haiku is concrete, common, and natural. Avoid words that are judgemental such as *gorgeous* or *wonderful*. Also avoid words that are abstract: *love, courage, loyalty*. Haiku is written in the present tense, although there are exceptions. Some haiku have no verbs.

Haiku depend upon the five senses. Something you can:

- *smell (garbage, a skunk, smoke)*

- *taste (blueberries, cold water, salty popcorn)*

- *hear (sirens, school bells, tv's)*

- *touch or feel (sand, thorns, a turtle's shell)*

- *see (the stars, slogan tee shirts, celebrity posters, the neighbour's cat)*

Haiku consist mostly, (although sometimes this may not be true) of two images put together to create harmony, contrast, emotions, depth. One image may appear on one line, the other image may be described in the other two lines, or vice versa. There should be a pause at the end of either the first or the second line, but not both. Sometimes you might find a comma, a dash, an ellipsis (...) separating the two parts of the haiku; however, it is not necessary to use punctuation.

Once you begin to compose more haiku about the nature around you, you will become more aware of seasonal changes and seasonal words (called *kigo* in traditional haiku) This guide book will give examples for techniques to improve the quality of your haiku, and to inspire more creative thinking, and writing.

After writing haiku about the self (these poems are often called *senryu*, but for simplification, they will be called *haiku:you*), it is important to look around, outside your "own" experience, and notice the community, nature, the cosmos, that is also a part of your larger world.

Part 5: Haiku techniques

Haiku is an art form, a poetry. The seven most popular techniques for writing haiku are:

- *Comparison*

- *Contrast*

- *Association*

- *Mystery (Yugen)*

- *Narrowing the focus*

- *The sketch*

- *Focus on the senses*

Comparison

a sky full of stars
how improbable
my parents would meet

Robert Mainone

A haiku needs two parts. In this haiku the "sky full of stars" is compared to "the meeting of parents" and the million-to-one chance of that happening. The poet has achieved an aha moment! with the connection.

Writing exercises

* *Using the poet's first two lines, add a third line of your own.*

* *Compose a haiku that compares two things that you like.*

* *Compose a haiku that compares two things that you don't like.*

After you have completed these "recipes" for writing, read the following haiku. What comes to your mind? Try moving out on your own.

the first chip
in our windshield
Northern star

Susan Constable

alone in Tokyo
even the chopsticks
in pairs

Terry Ann Carter

Contrast

gelled hair
perfectly in place
his anarchy t-shirt

Angela Leuck

The poet is contrasting the images of hair perfectly in place and a t-shirt that is advertising the idea of complete disorder. The humour is found in the juxtaposition of these two opposing "styles."

Writing exercises

- *Using the poet's first two lines, add a third line of your own.*

- *Compose a haiku that contrasts your personality with a friend's.*

- *Compose a haiku that contrasts you with your mother/father/sibling.*

Read the following haiku. What comes to your mind? Try creating one of your own.

this cold morning
I pull on my pants
hot from the dryer

Michael McClintock

sun sets
my ego continues
to shine

George Swede

Association

endless scales
on the neighbour's flute —
my mother's ironing

Dorothy Howard

The "endless scales" from the flute of the poet's neighbour is reminding the poet of her mother's endless chore of ironing. She associates the drudgery of scales with the drudgery of a household chore.

Writing exercises

- *Using the poet's model, compose a haiku that associates something you own with the lyrics of a favourite song.*

- *Compose a haiku that associates a particular place with the weather.*

- *Compose a haiku that associates a mood with a school subject.*

almost too rich
for the senses —
chocolate chip iris

Claudia Coutu Radmore

darkness
the only thing big enough
to hide an ocean

Claudia Coutu Radmore

Mystery (Yugen)

summer afternoon …
the first drops of rain
on my bare feet

Stanford M. Forrester

Sometimes, there is a moment that completely takes your breath away. Feeling that first drop of rain, so happy to be alive, outdoors, on a summer's day, so delighted to be part of the mystery of nature, the mystery of life. The poet is refreshed by nature.

Writing exercises

- *Using the poet's first line, compose two new lines to express an "ordinary" event from everyday living that might take place on a summer afternoon.*

- *Write haiku about the natural world, remembering moments from the seasons. Below you'll find some notes, some examples, and an in-depth look at one haiku poet to inspire nature poetry of your own.*

Haiku traditionally include a season word (kigo) such as blossoms, tadpoles, April Fool's day for SPRING—mosquitoes, fly swatter, fireworks, heat wave for SUMMER—pumpkins, falling leaves, harvest moon for AUTUMN—frost, hail, icicles, New Year's Day for WINTER.

A Close Up View of One Poet's Work: Grant D. Savage

*This is the perfect place to stop and consider the work of one particular poet —
in some depth. I have chosen poems written by Canadian haiku poet Grant D.
Savage; they have been collected according to seasonal references. Note
Grant's eye for detail, his use of exact names for natural images, his sense of
humour. See if you can determine where the pauses are, whether images are
being compared, contrasted, or associated. See if you can spot the sketch
(shasei).*

Autumn

> no snow yet
> trying to make angels
> in the leaf piles

> early morning pond
> reflected in its stillness
> everything

> goldenrod fading
> at the edge of the woods
> a doe pauses

> silent woods
> my fart
> flushes a grouse

> dull evening
> the only sunset
> autumn leaves

> wet dog smell
> the old newf sleeps unaware
> of the passing geese

Winter

first snow
the cat followed everywhere
by its footprints

unmelted
in the dead fox's fur
first snow

patches of snow
moonlight bounds away
on a buck's tail

Feb. 15th
mascara
on the roses

winter wind
a leaf rattles through
the waterfall's silence

psych ward
moonlight climbs
the walls

grey evening
only an owl's hoot
marks day from night

Spring

spring rain
finding myself
on her to do list

spring comes
to the old jalopy
brand new...rust

from reed to reed
a blackbird follows
            its song

late afternoon
tulips fill with shadows
of themselves

haze –
the distant hills
shape the afternoon

approaching storm
      showers me
           with white blossoms

Summer

bright morning
left clinging to a reed
dragonfly's old self

releasing a bass
its cool into
the river's cool

a red letter day
both rabbit and groundhog
eating my weeds

light in the wings
of the shadow
of a dragonfly

hiss of rain
onions sizzle
as they hit the pan

night of no moon
now and then a ripple
of loon laughter

Narrowing the focus

in the meadow
the cow's lips
wet with grass

Penny Harter

This is a "haiku technique" that the poet Buson used a great deal, for being an artist he wrote with an "artist's eye." Basically start with a wide angle lens on the world in the first line, switch to a normal lens for the second line, and zoom in for a close up in the third line.

Writing exercises

- *Use the wide angle lens technique to compose a haiku about a city street, a lake in cottage country, your own backyard. Start wide and gradually focus in on one object.*

Here is another example:

inside the box
sits a doll
shoeless

Noelle Egan

The converse is also true. Begin with a small image and move outward.

tattooed neck
of the stranger next to me
bridge graffiti

Terry Ann Carter

The sketch

> on the bus
> the teenager pulls out a mirror
> and adjusts her pout
>
> *George Swede*

The haiku "sketch" or "shasei" originated in Shiki's time, when the poet rebelled against the "rules" of haiku and decided to write simply what caught his eye (often with a bit of humour). The poet is not contrasting images or comparing images or associating images. A kigo (seasonal word) is not present.

Writing exercises

- *Sketch a scene from the school cafeteria, the school gymnasium, your dining room.*

Here are a few more examples of the sketch:

> science project
> Jupiter
> on the floor
>
> *Mark Wilson*

Sometimes the sketch may have a dark side...

> in front
> of the meth lab
> three children hopscotch
>
> *C.J. Welch*

Focus on the senses

metallic taste
the cold stream spills
from my hand

Jenny Zhang

shifting shadows
deep in the hills
a dog barks

Allison McCrossen

koi
nibbling
my copper wish

Elizabeth Hetherington

up a tree
among the green apples
girl in a red sari

Angela Leuck

autumn fog
the squeaking brakes
of a school bus

Lenard D. Moore

Writing exercises

- *Review the example haiku for their sensory detail: metallic taste, a barking dog, the girl in the red sari, and the squeaking brakes.*

- *Brainstorm ideas for a particular theme (e.g., the seasons, times of day, different landscapes) by listing details from all 5 senses.*

- *Collaborate on a class haiku using items from the list above. Then invite students to compose their individual haiku.*

Part 6: Tanrenga, Rengay, and Renga/Renku— Linked Haiku

Tanrenga

Tanrenga is a co-operative "linked" form of poetry. One student composes the first three lines and a second student "answers" with two lines. The answer is a link and a shift which means a "link" to the first three lines, yet a "shift" in the topic to something new. This technique, called "link and shift," is used in all forms of linking poetry — also in haibun, which will be discussed in the next chapter. Answers can be humorous, serious, playful, satiric. The most important point is use your imagination, be playful, have fun! Here are some examples of tanrenga by Canadian haiku poets Michael Montreuil and *Claudia Coutu Radmore*.

at what moment
does a cucumber
become a pickle?

> *every time elvis*
> *leaves the room*

* * *

Sunday dawn
our cats meow
from places unknown

> *some black holes*
> *we don't know about*

* * *

the national enquirer
says the world will end
in 2012

> *only a year*
> *to clean up my act*

* * *

her prom dress
without a single strap
to dangle

> *always a new strategy*
> *to be developed*

> * * *

Mattel sales down
Barbie Video Girl
gets a facelift

> *even newborn*
> *she doesn't look her age*

Rengay

Garry Gay invented the "rengay" in 1992. Here are some of his notes concerning this format.

To write a good rengay you are probably a good haiku writer. The rengay, like the haiku, relies on your ability at suggestive writing.

Let's look at the rengay's structure. For two writers the progression is as follows, with the letters representing the poets and the numbers indicating the number of lines in the given verses:

A-3, B-2, A-3, B-3, A-2, B-3.

The pattern for three poets is as follows:

A-3, B-2, C-3, A-2, B-3, C-2.

A rengay is a collaborative six-verse linked thematic poem written by two or three poets alternating three-line and two-line haiku or haiku-like stanzas in a regular pattern or form. It is really important to keep in mind that each verse is really a stand-alone haiku in either three or two lines. Many haiku writers don't write two-line haiku very often, so these can be the most challenging. Sometimes they are also the glue that holds the rengay together.

The rengay lets you explore a topic or theme, or stay in one place or season. They are very effective in celebrating a special occasion like a wedding or an event like the 50th anniversary of the Golden Gate Bridge.

There are a number of ways to approach the theme or central topic of a rengay. You and your writing partner can each suggest a theme you are interested in, like writing about birds or the color blue. Or you can take a walk or hike and write about some shared experience.

Linking and shifting can be quite fun in rengay. You can link back to the previous verse or link to the theme. Shifting needs the most care. While you can easily shift away from the previous link, if you shift too far away, the overall poem will not make sense. Some shifting will add natural tension to the poem. Some shifting will keep your writing partner guessing where you are going. Sometimes shifting away can be playful, but again, if you go too far you will lose your reader.

The fun part is talking over your verse or link. Does it communicate the mood of the poem? Did you use a similar word earlier? Did you advance the idea or concept of the poem?

The whole process of writing together is where the real joy and satisfaction comes. Remember that this is a collaboration.

The last link is a very important verse. Sometimes it links back to the first verse, but not always.

Sometimes there is a second theme or sub-level theme running through the poem.

This is an excellent site for rengay writing: http://www.baymoon.com/~ariadne/form/rengay.htm

Here is an example of a rengay composed by Terry Ann Carter and *Richard Straw*.

Breaking Point

"every toy has a right to break"
                        Antonio Porchia, Voices

dropped doll
her porcelain smile
all over the floor

        a winter skylight
        glass eyes stare at stars

trimming the tree
with hand blown ornaments
she tells war stories

burned out light bulb
he fumbles among boxes
in the attic

        cracked mug of chocolate
        the melting marshmallows

taillight shards
by a brick mailbox post
the moonlit ice

Note to teachers

The use of epitaphs from literature that the class might be studying is a strong motivation for writing rengay. It also lets students consider literary material in a new way, in their own creative approaches to interpreting the quotes.

Renga or Renku

Renga was a popular form of poetry in fourteenth century, Japan. Poets would gather and write a long, chain linked poem, each poet taking a turn adding two or three lines. Today, poems written in this style are often called renku. Here is an example of a kasen renga (36 links) composed by American poets Fay Aoyagi and Lenard D. Moore.

December Morning

(November 11, 2010 – December 5, 2010)

a kasen
by *Fay Aoyagi* and *Lenard D. Moore*

1 (winter)
> December morning
> a smart phone vibrates
> with another message   *FA*

2 (winter)
> a stranger with gloves
> on the station platform   *LDM*

3 (no season)
> a delivery truck drops
> an odd-shaped package
> at the hill-top house   *FA*

4 (no season)
> a streetlight pops on
> and then another one   *LDM*

5 (no season)
> slow night
> she fishes for chewing gum
> in her purse   *FA*

6 (no season)
> I pick up my blue shirt
> from the downtown cleaners   *LDM*

7 (cherry blossoms)
> cherry blossoms
> on my digital camera
> the setting sun   *LDM*

8 (spring)
> old lady hums
> a tea pickers' song   *FA*

9 (summer)
          sound of the river
          a firefly blinks
          above the parked car   *LDM*

10 (no season/love)
     she whispers her *yes*
     in her native tongue   *FA*

11 (no season/love)
          rubbing her shoulders
          in the middle of the night
          satellite jazz   *LDM*

12 (moon)
     a peacock feather
     in the moonlight   *FA*

13 (autumn)
          red letters on logs
          on the passing semi —
          gold leaves   *LDM*

14 (autumn)
     a harvest festival
     in full swing   *FA*

15 (no season)
          light bulb blows
          in the home office
          morning news   *LDM*

16 (no season)
     anchor woman
     and her hairdo   *FA*

17 (winter moon)
          winter moon
          I find the shirt I started
          in high school   *LDM*

18 (winter)
     snowbound
     with origami papers   *FA*

19 (no season)
          Monkey King
          and his body-doubles
          practicing kung fu   *FA*

20 (no season)
books lean the same way
on the new bookshelf   *LDM*

21 (spring)
first dandelions
we spot
during our walk   *FA*

22 (spring)
a woodpecker hammers
my neighbour's biggest pine   *LDM*

23 (no season)
insistent door bell
mother-in-law brings
his favourite dish   *FA*

24 (no season/love)
he carries her books
to their next class   *LDM*

25 (summer/love)
time share
in Martha's Vineyard
a ring under the pillow   *FA*

26 (summer/love)
our matching t-shirts
drying at the cottage   *LDM*

27 (moon)
tiny flags
on the bottled-ship
white day moon   *FA*

28 (autumn)
warming the last slice
of pumpkin pie   *LDM*

29 (autumn)
autumn's end
hickory scent
from the smoke house   *FA*

30 (winter)
all day drizzle
on the fallen leaves   *LDM*

31 (winter)
city night—
a sneeze erupts
ahead of us   *LDM*

32 (no season)
a bag lady
at the bus stop   *FA*

33 (cherry blossoms)	we recite sonnets on the park bench cherry blossoms	*LDM*
34 (spring)	a letter tied to a balloon slowly ascends	*FA*
35 (no season)	portfolios to be graded — another day	*LDM*
36 (no season)	a silver spoon at the estate sale	*FA*

We tried to follow "Kasen renku rules" which are basically as follows:

1.   Kasen (36 verses) have 4 sides. (In ancient Japan, renga poets use a special paper to write down their poems).

Side1: Omote (meaning "front") (#1-6) Except for hokku (first verse), no proper name, no death, no religion, no love here
Side 2: Ura (meaning "back") (#7-#18)
Side 3: Nagori-omote ("remaining front") (#19-30)
Side 4: Nagori-ura ("remaining back") (#31-36)

2. Three moon verses (usually #5 and #13, #29). The moon verse can appear before or after these "usual" places, but should be accompanied with autumn verses. (i.e.: If #5 is autumn moon, #6 should be autumn)
3. Two cherry blossom verses (usually #17 and #35). The blossom verse can appear before these "usual" places, but should not be after.
4. Love verses should appear twice (ideally somewhere in Side 2 and Side 3).
5. Spring and autumn verses should appear in verse #3 and #5 (usually three in a row); summer and winter verses 1 to 3 (usually 2) in a row. Seasons should not be backward (i.e.; NO spring before winter)
6. Same season or subjects should have enough room (3-5 verses) between them.
7. Link and shift (DO NOT repeat an image or subject that has appeared in the previous two verses) (i.e.; if #7 is about "beach," and #8 is about "summer house," #9 should NOT be about "sandcastle" or "ocean waves.")

These are some of the main rules that my Japanese renku masters taught me. Enjoy!   *Fay Aoyagi*

Note to teachers

If students are going to write a traditional kasen renga, these are the rules to follow. Remember, a renga/renku is not narrative. Students may wish to try a more relaxed form of linking by following ideas from Canadian renku master, Marshall Hryciuk (Toronto). Marshall relaxes the rules and sets out with an easier style. His main aim is for haiku poets to have fun.

In the poet's own words, "I would tell teenagers that renku is a listening game where the object is to go with the flow. Just re-imagine what the words mean from the last link, and write down the first image that appears while their eyes are still closed. Then, adjust it to the specifics of the leader's request: for example, spring, outside, two lines. It's a way of letting your right brain find language by itself. Let the leader be the left brain organizer. It's an organic mosaic."

Part 7: Articles of inspiration for teachers and students

The Haiku Roadshow

LeRoy Gorman

> between Short Story
> & Shakespeare
> a ~~haiku~~ moment

The regular English class is no place to teach haiku. Curriculum and time constraints work against any meaningful study. Haiku in this setting is usually reduced to a syllable-counting exercise. Taking the show on the road, however, by moving out of the routine schedule offers a chance. A half to full day workshop can be used to inspire and teach students to write haiku. In my experience, this roadshow approach works and can be readily conducted in three parts:

The Opener (exploring and reading haiku)
The Main Event (writing haiku)
The Closer (publishing haiku)

The Opener

Something hands-on works to break the ice. I begin with a game of Haiku Match-A-Line[1]. The game is easy to set up and administer. To prepare, select haiku by different authors (20 is a comfortable number) and duplicate on 3 X 7 cards with the author's name beneath each. Cut away the third line and author's name from the first two lines. Shuffle the pieces and give to students to reassemble. The process works best with small groups of three to five[2].

The game easily leads to an informal exploration of poetics and the nature of haiku. Follow-up discussion usually comes to three conclusions: haiku is short, haiku contains one or two word pictures (images), and haiku suggests rather than tells. From here, a short lesson on the history of haiku can be given followed by ways (a few) to present haiku other than in three lines (as seen in the game examples).

To illustrate options to the three-line format I discuss one-line, multi-line and visual-concrete presentations. To illustrate visual possibilities, I use some of my own poems. These include more accessible ones, such as the ones appearing on the following page.

S   N   O   W   F   E   N   C   E
after the blizzard   SsunNsunOsunWsunFsunEsunNsunCsunE
S   N   O   W   F   E   N   C   E

out of fall mist
                              a duck
        f

                                            e
                                            a
                                            t
                                            h
                                            e
                                            r

More in-depth explorations may include: one word haiku, word-melds, sound haiku, and language haiku. These are best left for later sessions after students have had some experience writing their first haiku.

The Main Event

With the basics, students are ready for the main event—writing their own haiku. The first step is to generate images. In an ideal world, it would be nice to go for a nature walk where images could be easily absorbed and put into poetry. For the roadshow, however, something more expedient needs to be in place. A method I find useful is one I call *The Paired-Opposites Shortcut to Haiku Images*. To proceed, first create a list of paired opposites, such as:

big	small
rich	poor
old	new
young	old
hot	cold
city	wilderness
dead	alive
wet	dry
quiet	loud
dark	light
war	peace
open	closed

Using the list, have students create an image for each word[3]. For example, "rich" / "poor" may result in "gold"/ "homeless person." Using the images created, students can then focus on one to three pairs to develop. Using a separate page for each, have students write the images at the top of the page followed by four versions and/or revisions of a haiku, as in the following:

gold / homeless person

1. golden leaves
    fall on the banker
    and the homeless man

2. the homeless man asleep

                            on leaves of gold

3. outside the bank
    the homeless man up to his ankles
    in golden leaves

4. the homeless man
    ankle deep in gold
    leaves

The process may need to be modelled and coaching given to get students through the first one.

Once students have written haiku for two or three of the paired images, the best version from each page of four may be selected. At this point, it may be decided that the poems are polished or that they are still works in progress requiring further attention.

Throughout, it is important to remind students to be brief and only use the best words. To assist, a checklist of questions, like the following, is useful.

7 Questions To Ask When Writing

1. Are there extra words?
2. Are the words the best (precise nouns and verbs, for example)?
3. Are the images clear?
4. Does the poem sound smooth or rough when read aloud?
5. Could the poem be written another way (as one line or as a visual poem, for example)?
6. Does the poem allow the reader to feel rather than tell what to feel?

7. Does the poem make sense?

Once the haiku are polished to suit, it is time to present to an audience.

The Closer

A poetry reading is the most straightforward way to present. It may be a simple reading of the poems, or reading with musical accompaniment. Alternatively, or in conjunction with reading aloud, haiku can be published in various formats including broadsides and online renderings. My preference is the poetry postcard. The format is practical and ideal for showcasing individual haiku.

To create a haiku postcard, inexpensive card stock cut into 4 X 6 pieces is ideal. Students can render their haiku on one side and have plenty of room on the back for an address, message, and stamp[4]. At this point, the poets are published, the job is done, the show is over.

On to the next Haiku Roadshow…

Notes

[1] I first learned the game from Dorothy Howard. It can also be adapted to for use with other short forms such as: tanka, sijo, sedoka, cinquain, limerick, and clerihew.

[2] With a class of twenty, four or more sets may be necessary. Since, in most cases, each group will have the same set, it may be advisable to generate the cards on a computer and print enough copies to make up a number of sets.

[3] Vocabulary may vary in level of difficulty depending on student readiness.

[4] Students may also be told of the rich history of mail art and encouraged to illustrate their haiku.

Literary Inspiration For Writing Haiku

Penny Harter

When reading or teaching a well-written piece of literature, I often find myself writing haiku or longer poetry as a result of the experience of having "entered" the story. In this piece, I'd like to offer some examples of haiku written as a result of encounters with well-known classics often taught in the secondary or college classroom. Some haiku purists have said that unless a haiku is born of the poet's actual experience, it is not a real haiku but a "desk haiku" (said pejoratively). I do not consider haiku born of our imaginative encounters with literature to be "desk haiku." Any acutely perceived moment which strikes us deeply, whether in our physical or imaginative lives, is a moment we have lived, and potential material for our own haiku or other writing.

Almost any text taught in secondary school or college contains potential haiku moments. We can look to the physical descriptions of setting, put ourselves into a character's place in a given situation, or animate the text imaginatively, adding some moments of experience or perception not in the original but tangential to it. Here is a haiku sequence I wrote as a model for my high school students, after reading *Grapes of Wrath*, reprinted from my collection *The Monkey's Face*.

Dust Bowl

hound running
between the rows
of shrivelled corn

a child
draws the sun
in the dust

rock-a-bye baby —
porch door swinging
in the rising dust

dust storm —
black corners
of the child's eyes

farm gone, the farmer
fingers the stubble
of his beard

picking crops
she wipes the blood
on her flowered dress

nightfall—
the coolness of dirt
between toes

through the cardboard walls
harmonica

Both *Macbeth* and *Hamlet*, Shakespeare's plays often taught in schools, offer powerful stimuli for recognizing haiku moments. While teaching *Macbeth*, I wrote a sequence, influenced by Shakespeare's imagery, in which I imagine Macbeth's state of mind after his murder of King Duncan:

Macbeth, after the murder

tonight—
no stars,
blood on the moon

my cracked lips bleed—
I cannot say amen
to bless his soul

outside his chamber
the wind howls the sound
of my name

my wife's face—
a grim ghost
floats in the dark

no sleep—
fever burns
my living flesh

> hooting, the owl
> digs sharp claws
> into my skull

> who will wipe the death sweat from his brow?

When I shared the sequence with my students, they were eager to try writing their own haiku responses both to that scene and to others in the play.

The character in *Hamlet* that I find most compelling is Ophelia. Hamlet, who has led her to believe that he loves her, suddenly insults her and turns on her, and after she finds out that he has killed her father, Polonius, she goes mad, eventually drowning herself. After her father's death, she says to her brother Laertes:

> There's a daisy. I would
> Give you some violets, but they withered all when
> My father died. They say he made a good end.
>
> (4.5.207 – 209)

From this I wrote:

> at the graveside
> she lifts one daisy
> from the coffin lid

> father dead, she fists
> a clutch of violets, drops them
> crumpled to the grave

Later, I imagine myself at the brook's edge, watching Ophelia slip into the water still grasping her woven crown of flowers, and wrote:

> grey willow leaves
> above her face, the colour
> of the sky

> my cold fingers
> release to the stream
> yesterday's blooms

If we know a Shakespeare play well, we may turn to any event or character we remember and write haiku inspired by Shakespeare's imagery.

Passage to India is another text often taught on the secondary and college levels. It moves slowly, with long passages of dialogue, and much philosophical musing. However, there are several parts of the book that offer fine haiku possibilities. One is the opening chapter, describing the city of Chandrapore. Another, reproduced below, is the description of the Ganges at night. Ronny, a young Englishman, is looking down on the river with his fiancée and his mother.

> *Their attention was diverted. Below them, a radiance had suddenly appeared. It belonged neither to water nor moonlight, but stood like a luminous sheaf upon the fields of darkness. He told them that it was where the new sand-bank was forming, and that the dark raveled bit at the top was the sand ....*

> *... The radiance was already altering, whether through shifting of the moon or of the sand; soon the bright sheaf would be gone, and a circlet, itself to alter, be burnished upon the streaming void. (p. 31)*

The following haiku, fairly close to Forster's imagery, came to me from this passage:

> at the river's edge
> the sand-bank, radiant
> as moonlight

To get started writing haiku inspired by a passage of literature, underline any words in the passage that move you. A reminder: in the world of imagination, we don't always have to tie our haiku directly into the given text. Have fun!

Haiku for ESL and Bilingual Teachers

Raffael de Gruttola

Teaching English to students from different countries can be most rewarding when students are exposed to the short form of haiku. The haiku allows the students to explore meaning in language at its most rudimentary yet revealing stage. They are able to capture essential moments in their lives and are excited to know that they can communicate with their friends and peers. This is accomplished by using the essential tools of grammar and at the same time exploring meaning from their direct experiences of Nature.

Using the shorter form of haiku with its simple rules, teachers are able to question the use of certain words and phrases and explore meaning from different perspectives. At the same time students become aware of the possibilities of language usage and how meaning can differ from one word to another. They will understand for example the differences in the very use of a simple definite or indefinite articles and why it is important to know what is specific and what is general in the meaning of their usage. With adjectives and modifiers they will learn the importance of the exact descriptive use of language and also that a simple prefix or suffix attached to a word can change the meaning and mislead the listener or reader.

All languages have their complexities of meaning. For example, the English language with its many diverse sounds for vowels and consonants can confuse the second language learner who may not be aware of the slight changes in meaning and spelling if a word is not used correctly. Since English is not a highly inflected language, meaning can shift easily from one phrase to the next since the rules for verb forms are not so complex as in other languages. On the other hand, second language learners can communicate meaning often with simple grammatically correct English language constructions with the use of a noun and verb. They also have fun with English idioms and all their peculiarities of meaning and structure.

The haiku poem and form can explore all the differences in the English language and convey a genuine feeling of emotion in such short phrases. For example:

> large hanging tongue
> no food
> hungry

The above haiku, though somewhat elementary in language usage, was written by a ninth grade Chinese bilingual student who was able to convey a sensation that she had a few hours before her lunch break.

Another example by a ninth grade student explored the use of punctuation which again can be a visual understanding of a condition or situation which otherwise might go unnoticed:

> "... ...?" "... ...!"
> who could understand
> what they say
> they are deaf

It's important to understand that the short haiku is a way to excite students about the possibilities of language usage without analyzing long or short sentences or paragraphs. This will come later in the students' development as they become aware of concepts and theories expressed in words. It's also important that they understand the affective use of language and how words can change attitudes.

> a pretty girl
> working in the garden
> the fragrance of flowers

The following poems were selected from an anthology published by the Massachusetts Association for Bilingual Education and appear here with permission.

> bloody arena
> filled with corpses
> eternal struggle
>
> *Vilayvanh Bounlutay* (Grade 12)

> a pig
> visits the market
> and never returns
>
> *Rem Doerk* (Grade 12)

> ugly duckling
> blossoming into a
> beautiful swan
>
> *Seangchanh Khamphanong* (Gr. 11)

Christmas is coming
I have something for you
my love

Hung Dao Tran (Grade 12)

mother checks
to see that we are well
mother deep in my heart

Diep Dinh (Grade 9)

Haiku of War and Peace (Ideas for Remembrance Day)

Rick Black

Can one find beauty in a land like Israel so laden with violence? In a land riveted by war yet striving so hard for peace? Indeed, one can—perhaps one must. Israel is both a beautiful and a violent land. I lived and worked there for six years, including three years as a reporter in the Jerusalem bureau of *The New York Times*. But I never felt like I was able to capture the essence of the country, its paradoxes and contradictions, in my reportage.

In 1991, I discovered haiku and realized that I had stumbled upon a form that I could use to write about the country in a way that I had always wanted. Like many post-World-War-II Japanese haiku poets, I did not only want to write about flowers and birds, or about natural beauty in and of itself. I needed to experiment with the interplay of the natural and human worlds, often incorporating missiles, tanks and other military weapons.

I found haiku hiding almost everywhere like thistles emerging from rocky outcroppings. I jotted down poems or intimations of them—a line here, an image there, and then revised them over and over again. Ultimately, these poems convey the stark images of Israel's landscape—images of peace and war, of hope and fear—and the way in which they blend together. They are both a protest against war and an attempt to live with the paradoxes of life in Israel.

In truth, I have always struggled to reconcile haiku's non-judgmental Zen-like approach to life with my own deep seated need to protest against life's injustices. I have an ongoing argument with God about the world's imperfections. By writing these poems, I have tried to put aside my protests for awhile and to savour life in all its mystery. I hope that they will help provide a glimpse into the "inner" life of the country and in some small way inspire hope in a region that is so in need of it.

> empty sandbox —
> a mortar shell explodes
> nearby harmlessly

> volley of gunshots
> teens keep playing soccer in
> the Moslem quarter

> on leave:
> a soldier's M-16 points at
> the Beatles poster

just buried soldier —
too soon for his mother to
notice the crocus

a sonic boom
sets off the car's alarm:
false prophecy

not yet abloom,
planted in army boots:
pink geraniums

is it a checkpost
or another star in
the night sky?

great blue herons
heading south like f-16's
autumn manoeuvres

two old veterans
revisit the battleground
arm in arm

rainbow's arc
the old city's domed rooftops
still glistening

For Teachers

Without strong writing models, haiku that are written for special days tend to turn into simplistic pieces—war is bad: peace is good. Rick's haiku show a strong juxtaposition of images: the mortar shell in the sandbox, the rusting vehicles beneath the cypress trees, a comparison of the flight of an f-16 and the blue heron. Conscious of word choices "autumn manoeuvres," "checkpost," "sonic boom," students should discuss these poems considering their images and a connection to nature. Using articles, photos or websites for stories or updates on present-day military activities in Afghanistan and Iraq—or, even better, interviewing a veteran in their family or community— students can be encouraged to write their own poems.

Haiku can be displayed on bulletin boards of poppies, military themed collages, newspaper articles.

Consonance as the Genesis of Humor in Haiku

Randy M. Brooks

I have always loved poetry—the passionate Greek lyrics of Sappho, the witty satire of Martial's epigrams, the quirky expression of Emily Dickinson, and the playful art of William Carlos Williams. These writers and their traditions engage me in a certain type of consciousness. But the joy of haiku—with its particular type of sensory humor based on being fully alive to each moment—took me over the edge into fanatical passion. I don't want to merely study or read haiku. I want to be consumed by haiku—to live, breath, eat, drink, write, revise, teach, publish, meditate on, enjoy and love haiku. Why? Because haiku is so alive, so fun, so creative, so playful, so very human.

Unlike most Western writing and poetry, haiku come from consonance instead of dissonance. The Western traditions of writing begin with disagreement and complaint—something is wrong, some injustice has occurred, someone has a problem, there is a conflict, a difference of opinion, a gap between what is known and unknown. The purpose of a novel or play or article or poem is to resolve some dissonance—to take us from problem to resolution. We expect characters to grow or change in a novel. We expect our readers to ask questions and to reach new understandings from an essay. Western poetry seeks to convey emotional insights into ourselves and our times.

But what does haiku ask of us? To be alive. To feel. To know this is the way it is. To enjoy the moment. To laugh. To enjoy this day's blessings. To remember. To dream in color. To remember with all of our sensory associations. To imagine being here and here and here again. It takes us from here to here again. Haiku doesn't resolve a thing! It solves no problems! Haiku don't ask us to change who we are. A haiku doesn't ask us to pretend we are someone other than ourselves. It has no utilitarian motives nor political purposes! It does not seek fame nor esoteric elite artistic status. If somebody tries to make haiku "work" these ways, it self-destructs into political aphorisms or witty social satire or self-important artistic manifestos, but it is no longer haiku. Teachers sometimes attempt to use it as an empty form to teach syllable counting, but they end up with "zappai" instead of haiku. Their students write traditional Western-poetry content based on witty dissonance or goofy jokes about spam instead of genuine haiku. Writers simply can't twist haiku to their own purposes, can't use it for self-expression, can't forge the haiku tradition into something else without losing the haiku itself. We love haiku because it has no purpose other than to be, to feel, to love life.

Now, I don't believe that every haiku has to be based on a moment of joy or only derived from fun situations. But I do believe that every haiku has within it a confirmation of the human heart being fully alive. We do find that vitality to be fun and invigorating, even when dealing with the darkest of moments. So for me the humor of haiku comes from a fundamental "consonance" — a sense of conveying an understanding and acceptance of things as they are lived. Haiku ask us to take time out from the troubles, the problems, the struggles, the workplace — time for fully being alive in the world, being in the felt joy of life. Consonance is the joy of haiku. It is the source of the humor of haiku.

The humor of haiku doesn't have to be slapstick nor witty, it can be as simple as this affirmation of being alive:

> wading through the fallen leaves
>   the boy looks up
> and laughs

Selma Stefanile
The Poem Beyond My Reach (Sparrow Press, 1982)

Haiku Slam and Beyond

Randy Brooks

The Millikin University Haiku Website (http://old.millikin.edu/haiku/) hosts projects, research, and publications for students, faculty and the haiku community. The website is an online learning community forum for publishing haiku studies, for supporting haiku-related scholarship and for expanding the haiku learning experiences beyond the physical limits of the residential campus. What you will find on the site:

- *speakers and readings*

- *student haiku projects*

- *student research on haiku*

- *haiku courses at Millikin University*

- *haiku competitions (haiku slam)*

- *published haiku by students*

- *teaching haiku*

- *student renga*

- *links to haiku websites*

- *directory of haiku magazines*

Also included is a haiku unit plan for secondary education by Molly Burns. The unit was developed as a project in Global Haiku Traditions at Millikin University, Spring, 2005. This two-week unit covers the basic forms of haiku (both American and Japanese traditions). The unit is designed to span ten fifty-minute class periods for Grade 9 or Grade 10 English classes. Each day's lesson is clearly outlined with thirteen appendix items: lesson handouts are included and are downloadable.

Haiku Cut: A Contemporary Poetry Slam Approach

The poetry slam is a popular contemporary approach to poetry competitions. Haiku poetry slams have also been popular, and I would like to report the approach I have developed from competitions and slams I have attended. While one approach calls for impromptu haiku written on the spot by competitors, in another approach the competitors bring a small "arsenal" of possible haiku for competition with the possible inclusion of some impromptu haiku in response to their competitors. If the judging is by show of hands or loudest cheers, then either approach tends to favor "shock value" or "pleasing the crowd" for winning haiku. I prefer an approach that allows competitors to use well-polished, previously written haiku in the competition.

Haiku Cut is coordinated by a master of ceremonies (MC), who calls the competitors to the stage, introduces them, and calls for first one haiku then the other. Then the MC calls for the votes and declares a winner of that round, continuing until a final champion is determined. Based on the example of Tazuo Yamaguchi, who served as slam organizer at the 2007 Haiku North America conference, the MC keeps score with balls on a peg board, so the crowd can see if the poet is close to reaching the number of wins necessary for that round. The MC contains the applause as necessary and keeps the competition moving along. Excerpts of the 2007 HNA haiku poetry slam are available on a DVD anthology, *Haiku: Art of the Short Poem*, produced by Tazuo Yamaguchi and published by Brooks Books in 2008.

Head-to-head individual competition — in this approach individuals line up on two sides of the stage. Each poet competes and either stays in the competition or is eliminated. The rounds can progress at different rates depending on the number of competitors. With lots of competitors the first round may be (1 out of 1) or (2 out of 3) to remain. With fewer competitors, the MC may start with 3 out of 5. As the rounds continue, the number of haiku required to win that round go up (3 out of 5), (4 out of 7), etc. so that poets need a depth of quality haiku to remain competitive beyond the initial rounds. Haiku may only be used once in a competition.

Team competition — teams of competitors prepare for the haiku cut, often based on possible topics known in advance. The teams bring their haiku for competition with each team offering one haiku per round. One team selects and reads a haiku then the other team selects and reads a haiku they think will beat it. The judges have flags to vote for the color matching the team headbands. Some of the rounds are based on prompts such as "siblings, spring, love, flood," that teams knew before the competition while others are impromptu "egg-timer" rounds with prompts for the team to write new, original haiku on the spot. I usually start with 90 second egg-timer rounds at first, then switch to one minute egg-timer rounds in the last competitions. I also include open-topic "mad-verse" rounds in which the teams may choose any haiku or senryu they would like to use.

Voting may be done by judges with flags (with colors matching competitor headbands). There are an uneven number of judges so that there are no ties in the competition. After hearing the two haiku (and repeating them if desired), the judges indicate their vote by raising the flag that matches the competitor's headband color. Alternative judging can be by the entire audience through cheers or show of hands. I prefer a combination of these two approaches with guest flag-judges deciding the advanced prompt rounds and the audience voting on the impromptu egg-timer and open mad-verse rounds. The tournament closes with two individuals or teams vying for the championship, usually with a best (5 out of 9) or (7 out of 13) championship round. As in all of my competitions, the winning teams receive haiku books for their awards.

Why compete? Because the performance and enjoyment of haiku are a fun, social way to participate in this engaging literary art. Writers learn which of their haiku are loved by readers, and readers learn to select quality haiku.

Youth and International Haiku

Rich Schnell

The International Haiku Conference & Festival 2008
Lake Champlain, Adirondack and Green Mountain Region of
New York, Vermont, Quebec and Ontario

Sponsored by:
Lake Champlain/ Adirondack Haiku Society
International Haiku Club
State University of New York at Plattsburgh

Three years in the planning phase, and ten years in the percolating stage,
the International Haiku Conference and Festival occurred July 29 through
August 2, 2008, and took place in Plattsburgh, NY; Burlington, VT and
Montréal, Québec. The festival & conference co-sponsored by the Lake
Champlain & Adirondack Haiku Society, the International Haiku Club, and
the State University of New York at Plattsburgh had three purposes: (1) to
cultivate regional identity among communities and especially youth; (2) to
foster new relationships between North American "North Country" artists
and International poets and artists, and (3) to expose and teach regional
youth about the haiku form and the consciousness that is associated with the
form.

To develop the youth format, the authors worked with several schools,
student representatives, and regional programs to involve youth in the
process. In addition, several teachers and youth specialists, and
representatives from Counselor Education, Nursing, and Literacy Education
were invited to participate in both planning and implementation processes.
This more concentrated planning occurred during the six months
immediately preceding the festival in the spring of 2008.

The Idea

The youth focused effort to be implemented was to invite both regional
and international poets to come one day early to the Lake Champlain region
for the purpose of teaching area youth about haiku and related forms. Poets
traveled from India, Japan, Ireland, and Canada and across the United States
in order to teach area youth about fundamentals of the haiku form, and also
about haiga. Most of the youths were teens enrolled in a special program
called Upward Bound, and were from Clinton, Essex and Franklin Counties
in Northeastern New York State, an area referred to as the North Country.

Day One

Approximately 30 students participated in these sessions which began with an overview of the International Conference & Festival, the objectives of the youth program, and the format for the Youth Day's activities. State University of New York Distinguished Service Professor, Dr. Rich Schnell (NY: US) provided a general overview of haiku and its primary characteristics based upon the work of R. H. Blyth, and contemporary regional poets. He stressed haiku's relationship with nature, and its characteristic as an "egoless" form of poetry.

After the initial lesson about haiku and its roots in nature, students gathered in small groups of three or four with international poets to "practice" the lesson, creating an initial verse. They shared these poems with poet facilitators and the other students in the group. They gave each other feedback, while the poet facilitator provided supportive, yet critical feedback regarding their work. Each small group explored what seemed to work with their poems, and the portions that did not seem to work.

After approximately 15 to 20 minutes of this activity, another poet, this time John Stevenson (New York), taught a lesson about haiku. He gave illustrations, and encouraged students to practice this new insight while writing in small groups. Once again student would share their work with an international poet, who would then provide feedback on their efforts. Twenty minutes later another poet such as Gabriel Rosenstock of Dublin, Ireland, John W. Sexton of Kenmare, Dr. Angelee Deodhar of Chandigarh, India and Claudia Coutu Radmore of Carlton Place, Ontario, presented additional dimension, provided haiku examples, and encouraged student to integrate new aspects. Again examples were provided, questions asked and answered, and a mini-practice session ensued. This process continued for approximately six sessions, broken up periodically with examples of haiga (haiku paired with a visual art form), in this instance photography, to convey the "Zen moment," of haiku insight. Students worked with different international poet/teachers to receive insight, and feedback.

As one of the closing activities, students and poet facilitators selected one poem from each of the youth, and—similar to the traditions at many haiku conferences—these emerging haiku poets shared their efforts with the audience. Each youth had an opportunity to stand in front of their peers and a group of accomplished international poets, to present their haiku poem, and experience audience feedback. This student haiku presentation lasted approximately 30 minutes.

For some teens this was a powerful and significant experience. Several youth came to the program having great challenges sharing their work aloud, either in school or in alternative learning environments; however, something about working with the haiku form, and also with experienced poets, permitted them to go beyond their previous barriers, and gratefully share their haiku efforts.

The English teacher coordinating the Upward Bound students had positive comments about the experience. She witnessed some significant breakthroughs as a consequence of the material and format. Also, the Executive Director of the Upward Bound Program, Ms. Elaine Leavitt, had very positive appraisals of the youth's experience at the day's "Youth Teaching Sessions."

The day's program culminated with Dr. Angelee Deodhar's (India) presentation on Children and Haiku. The presentation was a multimedia effort based upon work Dr. Deodhar has been carrying out with children from around the world, and their writing of haiku. Her presentation was especially well received.

Student evaluations of the event were positive: they enjoyed meeting the international poets, appreciated their time and efforts in helping them learn the haiku form, and improved their own sense of artistic expression through the medium of haiku. The international poets, likewise, had a positive experience, sowing the seeds for a future generation of haiku poets, who will better understand and appreciate "the way of haiku."

The Universe in Three Lines: Exploring New Worlds with Speculative Haiku

Deborah P Kolodji

When reading haiku, blank space on the page stimulates speculation. It engages the reader. A well-written haiku resonates, triggering memories of recognition. Speculative poetry takes this a step further, often painting a familiar scene in the context of an imaginary world. Speculative haiku is the unique juxtaposition between haiku and science fiction, fantasy, and horror.

Often called "scifaiku," speculative haiku is not new. In July of 1962, *The Magazine of Science Fiction and Fantasy* published six science fiction haiku by Karen Anderson.

> Those crisp cucumbers
> Not yet planted in Syrtis —
> How I desire one!
>
> *Karen Anderson* [1]

When read aloud, the alliteration of the first line, and the corresponding saliva the crisp "c" sounds produce, help me imagine the taste of cucumbers. I long for them, suddenly glad I live on a planet where they grow. A real experience is captured, even though the setting is imagined.

Sometimes a speculative haiku will create a contrast to a real experience:

> planet Valtec —
> every snowflake
> the same
>
> *Michael Dylan Welch* [2]

It is said that no two snowflakes are ever alike. A snow crystal might contain 10^{18} water molecules randomly scattered throughout the structure of the crystal. The probability that two such crystals would have the exact same layout is indistinguishable from zero. This is the experience of our world. But Welch writes of a planet, a place so alien that all snowflakes are alike. By focusing on a minute detail of an imaginary world, we come to visualize it better.

> green moonlight
> the engineer weeps
> over a letter from home

Joshua Gage [3]

We've all been away from home at some point in our life. Some of us further than others. Gage's speculative haiku captures the loneliness of being away from our loved ones. By hinting of an alien world in the first line, a place where moonlight is green, the sense of being very, very far away is magnified to the point that you fear the speaker may never be able to return.

> welcome home
> to this crater
> once bright Ithaca

dan smith [4]

What if Odysseus had returned to Ithaca to find it destroyed by a meteor? Haven't we all returned to a favorite place to find it changed, somehow for the worse? When I return to Long Beach, the city of my birth, I am always surprised when a familiar well-loved restaurant or store has been replaced by a new business. Again, Smith's imaginary scenario evokes a real emotion that we've all experienced and exaggerates it for emphasis.

So, what exactly is speculative haiku and how do you write it? In 1995, Tom Brinck posted "The Scifaiku Manifesto" on the internet, where he defined three essential elements. By his definition, a scifaiku should be a minimalistic science fiction poem, conforming to normal conventions of modern haiku. It should be immediate, written in the present tense, engaging the reader. Finally, it should convey human insight. The best science fiction is written about earthly events cast in a futuristic light as a parable to provide greater understanding. A year after "The Scifaiku Manifesto," the Scifaiku mailing list was born, a place where speculative haiku poets still gather electronically, often posting renga-like chains of scifaiku on a particular theme, for example "faster than light" travel.

> light speed
> a century ahead
> of his speeding ticket

Deborah P Kolodji [5]

In addition to bouncing ideas off like-minded souls on the internet, I enjoy starting with normal Earth seasonal words, then twisting them in different directions. At Haiku North America, I led an exercise using this approach, asking the audience for a summer kigo. David Lanoue suggested "sweat," which led to a variety of interpretations, including sweat in Zero G and rust on a medieval knight's armor. One of my favorites was this one by Naia:

> zero gravity . . .
> my beads of sweat floating
> among the stars
>
> *Naia*

Once you've written your first speculative haiku, what do you do with it? Some of the examples in this article were published in *Scifaikuest*[6], a poetry journal devoted exclusively to speculative haiku and related forms. *Star*Line*[7], *Dreams and Nightmares*[8], *Abyss and Apex*[9], *Astropoetica*[10], *The Magazine of Speculative Poetry*[11], *Tales of the Talisman*[12], and *Goblin Fruit*[13] are among the many science fiction, fantasy, and horror poetry journals that publish speculative haiku or tanka, often paying $1-$5 per poem for first rights. I have even seen speculative haiku, especially those of an astronomical nature, published in haiku journals.

In short, there's a whole galaxy of possibilities out there. I invite you to explore them with me.

Notes

[1] From *The Magazine of Science Fiction and Fantasy*, July 1962.

[2] From *Scifaikuest*, May 2008, Print Edition

[3] From *Scifaikuest*, August 2008, Print Edition

[4] From *Scifaikuest*, November 2008, Print Edition

[5] From *The Magazine of Speculative Poetry*, Spring 2006

[6] Scifaikuest, print journal and webzine (different content), edited by Teri Santitoro. http://www.samsdotpublishing.com/scifaikuest/cover.html, $6/issue, $20/4 issue subscription

[7] *Star*Line*, print journal of the Science Fiction Poetry Association, edited by Marge Simon, SFPA membership is $21/year US/Canada/Mexico, $25/year International. http://www.sfpoetry.com

[8] *Dreams and Nightmares*, print journal, edited by David C. Kopaska-Merkel, 1300 Kicker Rd, Tuscaloosa, AL 35404, subscriptions are $18 for 6 issues, $4 per issue

[9] *Abyss and Apex*, webzine, poetry editor—Trent Walters, http://www.abyssandapex.com

[10] *Astropoetica*, webzine, edited by Emily Gaskin, http://www.astropoetica.com

[11] *The Magazine of Speculative Poetry*, print journal, edited by Roger Dutcher, P.O. Box 564, Beloit, WI 53512, $19/4 issues, $5/sample issue

[12] *Tales of the Talisman*, print journal (poetry and fiction), edited by David Lee Summers, Hadrosaur Productions, PO Box 2194, Mesilla Park, NM 88047-2194, $24/4 issues, $8/1 issue.

[13] *Goblin Fruit*, webzine, edited by Amal El-Mohtar and Jessica Wick, http://www.goblinfruit.net

Haiku and Visual Art

Pamela Miller Ness

Ekphrasis is a technical term of Greek origin used by classicists and art historians to mean a verbal description of a work of art. The earliest known examples in the West date back to the ancient Greek poets, who developed a tradition of describing both imaginary and actual works of art. For example, Homer describes the fictional shield of Achilles, forged by the god Hephaestus, at great length in the 18th book of *The Illiad*. Many classical Greek lyric poets refer to works of art that scholars believe once existed but now are lost.

A similar ekphrastic tradition in the East dates back at least as far as the Heian period (794–1185) in Japan. Ki no Tsurayuki (c868–945) was a leading poet of the waka (early tanka) revival who wrote the preface and served as one of the editors of the *Kokinshu*, the first imperially-commissioned poetry anthology of 905. He wrote the following waka to describe a painted screen. (The translation is by Janine Beichman):

> Love-possessed, I went
> to seek my sister
> in the winter night
> and the river wind blew cold
> carrying the plovers' cries

The screen depicts winter, a cold river wind, and a man hurrying to his lover's house. The scene Tsurayuki presented here was to become almost an archetype in classical poetry.

Moving ahead seven centuries and into the haikai (haiku) tradition, we find several examples of ekphrasis among the hokku (haiku) of Bashō. This example is translated by Makoto Ueda, and the image of the poet is an 1892 woodblock after an ink portrait by Takebe Socho (1761–1814):

> my horse ambles along ...
> I see myself in a painting
> of this summer moor

This hokku was written in 1683, the year that Bashō's hut burned to the ground in a fire that destroyed extensive sections of Edo (an older name for Tokyo). According to Makoto Ueda, this disaster reaffirmed Bashō's belief that man was an eternally homeless creature. Bashō may have been looking at an actual painting and written himself in; or, while ambling on horseback across a summer moor, he may have imagined himself in the painting.

Two hundred years later, Masaoka Shiki also wrote about art, including several haiku about the act of painting. This haiku, written in 1902, the last year of Shiki's life, was published in *Stray Notes While Lying on My Back*:

> I thought I felt
> a dewdrop on me
> as I lay in bed

A head note explains that Shiki might have been looking at a scroll with a flower sprinkled with dew; the poet might have felt himself pulled into this world. The haiku attests to the extraordinary power of art to heal.

A Gallery of Contemporary Haiku and Visual Art

I think that poets write from works of art for the same reasons and following the same process they use to write from nature or direct experience: the poet observes closely and at length, enters into the world of art intellectually and emotionally, and allows the work of art to trigger some kind of epiphany. The poet may respond to the artist's imagery, colour, form, medium, technique, or style. The work of art is sketched in words, a process similar to Shiki's principle of *shasei*, or sketch from life.

A. Shasei: sketching juxtapositions internal to the work of art

Shiki borrowed the term "sketch from life" from the vocabulary of Western art to describe a technique of composing haiku based on minute observations of nature, in which mood is created through the manipulation of images. I believe that we can apply the same process to a haiku poet sketching works of art with words because the poet must observe closely, select which images to juxtapose and in which order, and carefully choose language.

> Tai chi class
> the seagulls also
> in formation

My haiku is a fairly literal verbal sketch of Wu Jialin's photograph taken in 1997 in the Yunnan Province of China, which was part of a photography exhibit at the Asia Society in 1999. I was struck by the photographer's juxtaposition of Tai chi practitioners and sea gulls in an urban park, a contrast that suggests the inherent similarities and connection between the human and natural worlds.

In the next haiku, Elizabeth Searle Lamb responds to the medium and technique of art rather than imagery:

shimmering beneath the glaze,
blue brush strokes
on the Chinese ginger jar

In her haiku based on Henri Rousseau's 1907 oil painting "The Snake Charmer," Alexis Rotella captures both the harmony of imagery (this is a world in which nature, animals, and humans are at peace) and of form by focusing on the round, white shape of the moon reflected in the snake's eye.

Jungle silence
white moon
in the snake's eye

Similarly, I was struck by the juxtaposition of shades of white and light in John Singer Sargent's large oil painting "Carnation, Lily, Lily Rose," and tried to capture that in my haiku.

lilies at twilight
lighting Japanese lanterns
two small girls in white

The next two images are from Hiroshige's "One Hundred Famous Views of Edo," a series of woodblock prints created between 1856—1858. The first depicts an evening scene with pleasure boats on the Sumida River set off by the famous landmark, the Pine of Success. I was inspired to write the haiku by observing the two pair of shoes and learning from the detailed label that a silhouette of a woman's upper torso can be discerned behind the green blind of the boat. I became intrigued by the mystery surrounding the two lovers whose only trace is their shoes in the bow.

summer stars
in the sailboat bow
two pair of shoes

Patricia Neubauer wrote her haiku

bright New Year's moon
ghost foxes gathering
under the thorn tree

about the final image in Hirosheige's series, the only print among these direct observations that involves fantasy. In this print, Hiroshige ventures into the world of spirits. According to Japanese legend, all the foxes of the eight Knato provinces gathered at a particular tree near Oji Inari Shrine with flames issuing from their mouths, flames by which farmers were able to predict the year's crops. Drawn again to the light, Pat sketches the scene fairly literally, until one notes that she has interpolated the moon or possibly seen its image in Hiroshige's title shikishi.

B. Juxtaposition of the work of art and immediate, direct response

A second type of juxtaposition that a haiku poet may make is between the work of art and an experience external to the work itself: perhaps an experience that occurs in the art museum while viewing the work. The following haiku reflect moments between the world of the art object and that of the viewer:

> Shoulder to shoulder —
> museum goers admire
> Hiroshige's crowds
>
>> *Claire Gallagher*

> open mouthed
> behind museum glass
> samuari's war cry mask
>
>> *Randy Brooks*

In her haiku based on van Gogh's "Sunflowers," Sister Mary Thomas is probably looking at the print in her own room or someone else's room and makes two juxtapositions: the contrast between the painter's lush flowers and her own empty vase and the similarity, perhaps comforting, between the abandon of the flowers and the fact that the print is askew on the wall.

> Her vase empty
> van Gogh's "sunflowers"
> askew on the wall

The following haiku, written by Gerard John Conforti during one of his confinements in a psychiatric ward, juxtaposes art and immediate experience with humour, irony, and great empathy.

> the psych ward's hallway
> paintings along the wall
> by van Gogh

C. Juxtaposition of a work of art to memory

Just as immediate experience can trigger an association to a work of art, a work of art can also bring up a personal, cultural, or literary memory. Georgia O'Keefe's "Black Cross" evokes for Elizabeth Searle Lamb an experience of the desert winds across the New Mexico desert.

> O'Keefe's "Black Cross"
> the wind blows and blows
> in the high desert

For Peggy Lyles, Picasso's whimsical baboon with a toy car on its head brings to mind a memory of her husband's beloved childhood toy.

> Picasso's baboon
> my husband describes
> a toy he loved

> Among these lilies
> in Monet's pond
>   Bashō's watersound
>
> *Sylvia Forges-Ryan*

D. Art triggers personal emotion

Just as direct experience and nature often trigger the emotional response that leads to a haiku, so, too, can a work of art serve as a catalyst for empathy, defined by Webster's as "The power to enter into the emotional harmony with a work of art." This phenomenon is illustrated by Nancy Morrey's haiku inspired by Picasso's 1902 canvas "Woman with Bangs."

> No glass
> between Picasso's Blue Period
>   and mine

Edvard Munch's famous painting "The Cry" (1893) inspired emotional response with a direct reference to the painting and a juxtaposition of the aural "no sound" with the visual scream in Sister Mary's haiku.

> No sound
> "The Cry" of Munch
> Pierces my ears

And a different response from Pat Neubauer:

lurid sunset…
from the woman on the bridge
a dark red scream

E. Art triggers imagination

Finally, just as art can trigger a juxtaposition with immediate experience, memory, or strong emotion, art can also lead the poet into the realm of fantasy. In the case of the following haiku, I tried to capture in words the artist's fantastical leap from the real world to the realm of fantasy

old scroll:
out of Fuji's mist
just the dragon's nose

In this brief overview of haiku inspired by works of art spanning two millennia, I hope you can see how a poet can approach a piece of art. By observing closely and entering the canvas or sculpture, the poet becomes open to a tiny epiphany, and finally, with carefully chosen words, makes a juxtaposition of internal elements, linking the image to immediate experience, memory, emotion, or imagination. I would like to leave you with some suggestions for using art as inspiration for your own haiku.

1. Describe the work of art, including a juxtaposition of images (*shasei*).
2. Enter the painting. Let the imagery or artist's technique trigger an emotional response.
3. Let the work of art trigger a memory; juxtapose the work of art to a personal memory.
4. Juxtapose the work of art to a well-known haiku or other piece of literature.
5. Let an immediate observation trigger the memory of a work of art or an artist's style.
6. Use the art work as a jumping off point for your imagination.
7. Juxtapose the work of art with an immediate observation.
8. Write a haiku about an experience in an art museum.
9. In a haiku or a tanka, address a figure in a work of art.
10. Write a haibun that includes reference to a work of art.
11. Write a haiku series or solo renga about one or more works of art.
12. Collaborate with others on a renku related to a work of art.
13. Write a series of haiku about a series of works of arts (for example, Hokusai's views of Fuji).

Books, Books, and More

Terry Ann Carter

Once you have a collection of haiku on a particular theme or subject, a small handmade book is an alternative to the notebook page, the computer file, or homework assignment. The small handmade book is also a perfect gift to give to yourself — or to others.

There are many styles of books: flutter books, accordion books, origami books, match box books, fan books. Later, with more practice, there are pop up books, spiral books, and books using all kinds of architectural design. The opportunities are endless. (I once made a "fairy book" with two halves of a walnut shell, hand drilled and wired together.) Recycled materials can also be used for interesting books: business envelopes often have a vellum window that will "show through" to a new title, and collages using text from a haiku make original covers for books. Hand sewn folio books (3″ x 5″ and 4″ x 6″) need waxed thread for binding, while more intricate Japanese "stab binding" may be used for larger books. Bindings can appear on the left side of the book (Western design), right side of the book (Asian design), or in a diagonal design which leaves both the upper side and lower side open for text. Tibetan books have no binding at all; sheaves of paper are simply tied with raffia, ribbon or wire; scroll books roll their way across a table top or floor. Small scroll books can be made from rolls of paper used for adding machines (inexpensive and available at office supply stores).

Flutter Book

The easiest book to make is the Japanese flutter book which uses only one sheet of paper. These small books work from the concept of folding, then cutting part of the folds to open a single sheet of paper into a "small book." The cuts cause the paper to develop unusual formations that are sometimes complex, similar to mazes.

Materials: one sheet of photocopier paper

Tools: scissors and craft knife

Process for the single cut maze:

1. Fold a sheet of paper in half lengthwise.
2. In quarters crosswise.
3. Then open it again. Cut down the centre with a craft knife or scissors.
4. Cut across the centre for two quarters of the sheet.

5. To form the book, gently pinch the two centres on either side of the cut.
6. Gently pull them apparent and down.
7. Then shape the paper into accordion-style folds to make a book.

Fold Book

Most common among fold books are those with accordion folds. This zig-zag shaped fold is also called a concertina or leporello. Fold books may be rectangular, square, or triangular in shape. These books have accordion-folded pages with separate covers both front and back. Because the text paper is quite soft, the covers must provide sufficient stability for the book to stand. That means the covers must be made of something exceptionally thick. Foam board is recommended for this purpose because it's thick yet lightweight.

Materials:
- text: any calligraphic rice paper available in a roll, cut as described below
- endpapers: one piece of photocopier paper or other inexpensive paper, cut in a square
- cover boards: one piece of foam board, cut in the same size as the endpaper
- ribbon (optional): grosgrain, satin ribbon, or cotton crochet tape—also raffia, light steel wiring, embroidery threads, metallic threads
- scrap paper for pasting or collage
- glue sticks
- scissors
- ruler

Tools:
- mat knife or craft knife
- metal straightedge
- bone folder or similar device for folding paper
- book press or large heavy weight

Process:

1. Cut a piece of the calligraphy paper eight times as long as it is wide. To make a smaller book, the paper may be cut in half lengthwise.
2. Start with the text paper stretched in front of you horizontally. Holding one end against the work surface, fold the paper down to make a diagonal fold.

3.   Now fold the long end of the paper up. Again, the corners must be perfect.

4.   Fold across to the left. Make a perfect corner again. This time match the bottom edges.

5.   Fold across to the right. Again, making a perfect corner.

6.   Repeat the folding sequence—down, up, right, left, right—until you've finished. If there is any excess paper at the end, trim it off.

7.   Glue the first page inside the front cover, and the last page inside the back cover. Wrap the book in waxed paper and cover with a paper weight.

The "more" in my title refers to small haiku banners or prayer flags. These "banners" are made with commercial adding machine paper and bar-be-que skewers. A roll of white adding machine paper is unfurled for about a foot and then torn in a diagonal pattern. The paper is flattened under a heavy book or ironed. After writing one, two or three haiku on the paper, (use your imagination to collage the haiku with small bits of ephemera), pierce the top with a wooden bamboo skewer. The white paper should be in the middle of the skewer. Bits of raffia, long narrow strips of coloured tissue papers, or hand made Japanese papers can "fly" alongside the haiku. These charming banners may be hung indoors or outdoors when the weather is complementary. In time, the outdoor banners will fade with the sun and rain, and eventually the haiku itself will disappear. I like to think that the haiku have gone back into the cosmos from where they came.

There are some wonderful books to help inspire creative book making. These are my favourites:

Cover to Cover: Creative Techniques for Making Beautiful Books by Shereen La Plantz

Bookcraft: Techniques for Binding, Folding and Decorating to Create Books and More by Heather Weston

Making Handmade Books: 100+ Bindings, Structures, & Forms by Alisa Golden

The Penland Book of Handmade Books: Master Classes in Bookmaking Techniques by Lark Books

Book+Art: Handcrafting Artists' Books by Dorothy Simpson Krause

Re-Bound: Creating Handmade Books from Recycled and Re-Purposed Materials by Jeannine Stein

Bookworks by Sue Doggett

Why Haiku: A Student's Perspective

Sherry Zhou

Grade 8, Croft House, Vancouver

It all began four years ago, when I was nine years old. My dad saw that there was going to be a workshop on haiku by Michael Dylan Welch. At that time, I loved writing all sorts of poems and my dad thought it would be cool to learn more about haiku. He dragged me to the workshop at Vancouver Central Library on that chilly March night, but after participating in the workshop (which included reading my most recent book of poems), it paid off. I emailed Michael five days later, asking him about where I could join clubs and submit poems. He told me that I could join Haiku Canada and submit haiku to the Vancouver Cherry Blossom Haiku Invitational. At the workshop, I also met Vicki McCullough, who invited me to participate in the Cherry Blossom Ginko at Queen Elizabeth Park, where I met Helen Baker and Terry Ann Carter. At the end of the ginko, Vicki invited me to join the Pacific-kana haiku club. From that moment on, I spent more time experimenting with haiku on the weekends. By December, I had my first submission to the Vancouver Cherry Blossom Festival. In 2009, Alice Frampton introduced me to Edward Zuk, who had judged haiku from Vancouver Cherry Blossom Festival in 2008. She wanted to find a pen pal my age, but instead, she found Edward, who became my mentor through emails. Edward has encouraged me to write different types of poems and he has helped me write stronger, clearer, and more descriptive poems (and still does) through comments on poems that I wrote and emailed to him.

I love writing haiku because it challenges me to write something inspiring in three lines using precise language. To me, haiku is a snapshot of a great moment, captured perfectly. Writing haiku allows me to express moments of awe, fear, hatred, love, and much more. It is like a breath of fresh air when I'm done. I write haiku as a hobby (generally, poetry is my real hobby, but I spend my time mostly on free verse and haiku).

Writing haiku gives back lots. It can improve your writing skills in language arts and increase your creative thinking. It allows you to improve your haiku skills as you practice more. Also, it could allow you to pick your best to submit in a contest. As well, it could give you recognition within a group as a poet.

Some writing tips that I find helpful:

When you write haiku, you must have a goal, no matter how small it seems. Your ultimate goal to writing haiku could be winning a haiku contest.

Carry around with you a pocket notebook, just in case inspirations pop into your head. It is always a good idea to jot notes down about topics for writing haiku.

If you have a so-called writer's block, take a walk outdoors. Look for interesting images that may help you.

You don't always have to write in 5-7-5 style. Sometimes it helps to write in different styles. In Japanese, it is traditionally written in 5-7-5, but English words tend to be longer, so it is flexible.

For example, here is a haiku Matsuo Bashō wrote in Japanese:

> furu ike ya —
> kawazu tobikomu
> mizu no oto

This haiku was written in 5-7-5 style. My favourite English translation of this haiku goes like this:

> old pond —
> frog jumps into
> sound of water

This translation isn't in 5-7-5 style, but both the rhythm and description sound close to the original. This is why it isn't always necessary to write in 5-7-5 in English, no matter how hard your teacher tries to convince you. ☺

When you want to indicate a pause at the end of a phrase, use a dash (–) so it is clear that a line has ended. For example, here is a haiku I wrote:

> cherry blossoms —
> petal after petal
> the only movement

Here, the dash signifies that "Cherry blossoms" is a line not directly connected to the next phrase.

Reread, revise, and edit your haiku. Every time you revise it, it could improve and have deeper meaning to you.

Here is another example I wrote a while ago:

> summer morning —
> I wander out
> of my dreams

If you join a haiku group, the members are very kind and encouraging, giving you good advice on how to write better haiku. I love writing haiku; it is one of my favourite hobbies. I hope that writing haiku can become one of your favourite passions, too.

Literacy, Haiku, and the Environment:
Perspectives from a Teacher-Librarian

Urszula Gesikowska

The library is the hub of a school; it is the center of learning for students, staff, and visitors. With a team of teachers, I participated in a Cooperative Literacy project for one full academic year (September to May). The project goal was to promote literacy through reading, writing, and oral communication. Our theme was The Environment.

The following strategies were put into place: each month would concentrate on an environmental "action." September—recycling, October—pollution, November—deforestation, December—water crisis, January and February—endangered plants and animals, March—energy crisis, April—environment and technology, May—disposing of waste.

Our list of events included: displays in the library "Earth is Our Only Home"; environmental literary works read in the classroom; P.A. system presentations: songs and poetry; articles about environmental issues posted in classrooms; environmental prayers; presentations based on "An Inconvenient Truth"; Environmental Issues debate (held in the library); "keepers of the earth" Native stories and environmental activities; haiku poetry presentations (held in the library) with poetry readings, book making, haiku banners, haiku prayer flags, and a poetry contest; green lunches; and writing competitions.

The haiku writing workshop incorporated ideas from all the other presentations by using images of the earth, images of nature. Other resources included books and posters, art supplies, artifacts, photographs, and music.

The art of the small poem, capturing the aha! moment, added a new perspective this year. The workshops were accessible to students and teachers alike; the library became a meeting place for creativity, action, responsibility. My commitment to literacy, to the environment, to art and poetry is continuing.

2010 Haiku Invitational Winners: A Judge's Perspective

Michael Dylan Welch

Each year the city of Vancouver hosts an International Cherry Blossom Festival that includes music, street performances, workshops, poetry readings, and competitions for photography, art and poetry. The Vancouver International Cherry Blossom Haiku Contest includes a "youth division," which is of prime importance to teachers and students. This year the top five poems were read at a spring 2011 performance of the Vancouver Symphony Orchestra, and appeared soon thereafter on TransLink buses and SkyTrains in and around Vancouver, British Columbia. Their website lists many additional Sakura Award and Honourable Mention poems that you can also enjoy plus directions for entering the contest next year (http://www.vcbf.ca). Congratulations to all the winners, and thanks to everyone who entered for helping to celebrate spring and cherry blossoms.

Best British Columbia Haiku

biopsy . . .
but just for today
cherry blossoms

> *Laryalee Fraser*
> *Salmon Arm, British Columbia*

In the Japanese tradition, cherry blossoms are the supreme symbol of life's fleeting, ephemeral nature. In this case, the blossoms offer respite from life's sometimes harsh reality. Despite a biopsy, and whatever unwanted news that procedure might bring, the poet finds relief from her anxiety upon seeing cherry blossoms. Nineteenth-century agriculturalist Donald G. Mitchell has written that "I love better to count time from spring to spring; it seems to me far more cheerful to reckon the year by blossoms than by blight." This poem brims with optimism that we can only hope will spill into the future and not remain for today only.

Best Canadian Haiku

holding hands
for the first time
cherry blossoms

> *DeVar Dahl*
> *Magrath, Alberta*

Romance may well be the impetus for two people in this poem holding hands for the first time, or there may be many situations other than romance. Whatever the case, the magic of the blossoms has inspired two viewers to hold hands, and thus commemorate the moment of enjoying the blossoms as a *shared* moment. This is a poem of joy, and also a poem of *shared* joy. Sharing is one of haiku's goals, too, as the poet imparts his or her moments of perception and feeling to the reader.

Best United States Haiku

a sudden hush
among the children
cherry blossom rain

> *Melissa Spurr*
> *Joshua Tree, California*

It is easy to imagine children playing loudly and enthusiastically, no doubt heedless of the beauty of cherry blossoms around them—until a gust of wind, or perhaps just a breeze, causes a shower of blossoms to flutter down among them. The children are momentarily captivated, and thus become quiet. At such moments, too, don't we all become children, reveling in the wondrous beauty of nature? Here, too, we can equate the fleetingness of cherry blossoms with the fleetingness of childhood.

Best International Haiku

cherry trees in bloom —
if only I could stop
the wind

>   *Lucas Garczewski*
>   *Poznan, Poland*

Cherry blossoms are more beautiful because we know how briefly their beauty survives. Here the poet expresses a desire to sustain their beauty by wishing to stop the wind. And yet, despite this wish, we can see that a wind has swept through the cherry trees, setting blossoms to flutter down to the ground. In this poem we see a clear image and also see through a window into the poet's mind, and his yearning for the beauty of cherry blossoms to linger. Yoshida Kenko once said that "Blossoms are scattered by the wind and the wind cares nothing, but the blossoms of the heart no wind can touch." This is a poem that speaks of the heart.

Best Youth Haiku

the inspiration
for my wardrobe choice today —
pink cherry blossoms

>   *Rukshila Dufault, age 17*
>   *Port Coquitlam, British Columbia*

This poem salutes the changing of seasons to spring, where vibrant blossoms make the poet aware of the colour pink after a possibly drab winter. She is thus inspired to wear pink herself. The blossoms not only inspire but validate her choice. Perhaps, too, her wardrobe choice validates the cherry blossoms, or we might say that her choice *recognizes* the cherry blossoms. Cherry blossoms may ask no more of us than simply to recognize that they exist, as fleeting as they may be. But this is no small gesture, recognizing not only our relationship with nature, but even, at times, our identification with it.

Perhaps Rukshila's poem might encourage other students to enter the International Festival. I look forward to reading your poems in the future.

Old Pond Comics

Jessica Tremblay

http://oldpond.voila.net

Old Pond comics feature the adventures of Kaeru, a young frog who becomes the apprentice of master Kawazu, the wise frog who inspired Bashō's famous haiku *"old pond / a frog jumps in / the sound of water."*

Around 2006, I stumbled upon a website that listed 31 different English translations of Matsuo Bashō's frog haiku. Every translator was injecting a personal meaning into the poem. Did the frog jump or dive? Did Bashō mean to write "the sound of water" or "splash"?

"Well," I thought, "The only ones who knew what really happened at the pond that day were Bashō and the little frog."

That's when my imagination went wild. What if the frog who inspired Bashō thought that she had contributed to Bashō's haiku to the point that they should share writing credits? Such a frog, having co-written the world's most famous haiku, would surely consider herself a great haiku master and would feel entitled to open her own haiku school. The idea of Master Kawazu and a young apprentice Kaeru was born.

Kawazu is the ancient Japanese word for "frog." It's the word Bashō used in his original poem (*kawazu tobikomu, a* frog dives in). Master Kawazu believes a haiku should have 17 syllables, follow the 5-7-5 rule and contain a season word.

Kaeru means "frog" in contemporary Japanese. As an apprentice, Kaeru will learn the rules of haiku to later break them! He loves modern haiku and doesn't necessarily follow the traditional rules of haiku.

Old Pond was published for the first time in 2007 and has been appearing in *Gong*, the journal of the Association Française de Haïku, ever since.

In 2010, Old Pond was published in English for the first time in the haiku journals *bottlerockets* and *Frogpond*.

The website http://oldpond.voila.net features a weekly comic, a free calendar of haiku contests, and popular information such as rules, advice for writing haiku, masters of Japanese haiku, and more fun at the pond! Also available in French at http://vieiletang.voila.net

Part 8: How to incorporate haiku into school projects

- books: folding accordion, flutter books, fan books, pop up books

- recycled materials/book format

- poetry sculpture

- school calendars

- haiga for posters

- wall murals

- haiku banners and prayer flags

- environmental posters

- earth day awareness activities and festivals

- world day posters

- haiku / peace gardens

- memorial gardens for deceased students

- haiku engraved into stones

- stone gardens with haiku signposts

- creative writing contests

- poetry readings / cabaret

Part 9: A short history of haiku

It is believed that haiku evolved from a longer poem called the renga, which is a type of linked verse, common in Asian literature, but non-existent in the West. In the creation of a renga, a group of poets work together to create a poem. A renga begins with one poet composing a verse of 5-7-5-syllables; the group then adds alternating links of 7-7 and 5-7-5 syllables to the opening verse. This type of composition was a popular social event in Japan, and many complicated rules about what could or could not be included made it a challenging exercise for all involved. The opening 5-7-5 verse of a renga was called a haikai-no-renga. Eventually, the haikai-no-renga were written as independent poems. These poems were called haikai. In the 19th century, the poet Masaoka Shiki coined the term "haiku" to describe the 5-7-5 poem. (It is important to remember that English language haiku are composed with 17 syllables or less.)

Early Masters

Matsuo Bashō (1664 — 1694) was the first poet to raise haiku into a serious art form. Before this time, haiku were usually written as witty poems without any deeper meaning. Bashō's major contribution was to discover how haiku could be used to express sombre moods and a deep insight into life. Once, when visiting the site of a famous battleground, he wrote:

> Summer grasses —
> all the remains of
> a warrior's dreams

Bashō was also the greatest writer of haibun (prose and haiku combined).
His travel journals, especially Oku no Hosomichi, or The Narrow Road to the Interior, are among the masterpieces of world literature.

Yosa Buson (1716 — 1783) was also a painter; he brought to haiku an exquisite aesthetic sense. His ability to paint a picture in a few words has captivated generations of poets:

> a bush warbler singing
> its small mouth
> open

Those interested in Japanese art should seek out Buson's paintings, especially those that illustrate his haiku.

Chiyo-ni (1703–1775) is Japan's most famous female haiku master. A student of Bashō's two disciples, she worked in an age when haiku was largely a male domain. As a poet, painter, and Buddhist nun, she lived a vibrant life while creating poems of crystalline clarity and delicate sensuality.

> woman's desire
> deeply rooted —
> the wild violets

Kobayashi Issa's (1763–1827) incredible popularity in Japan comes from the circumstances of his life. His extreme poverty and sufferings, described in his journals, have gained the sympathy of generation of readers. He also showed a deep love for children and small creatures:

> a giant firefly
> flickering
> passes by

Masaoka Shiki (1869–1902) helped revive haiku at a time when it had become stagnant and encumbered with meaningless rules. Shiki coined the term "haiku" and strove to raise it to the artistic heights it had enjoyed earlier, in the time of Bashō and Buson. His haiku often reveal a surprising combination of images:

> the pear blossoming …
> after the battle this
> ruined house

Shiki is also famous for his critical essays in addition to his poetry.

More historical information and examples of poetry may be found in the resources listed at the conclusion of the haiku chapter.

Haiku in America

In 1913, Ezra Pound's now famous "In a Station of the Metro" was published in *Poetry* magazine.

> The apparition of these faces in the crowd;
> Petals on a wet, black bough.

Other poets followed in an imagist tradition: Wallace Stevens, William Carlos Williams, Amy Lowell, Charles Reznikoff.

When the distress of World War II began to clear, two important haiku interpreters found themselves in Tokyo. Harold G. Henderson was on the staff of the American occupation forces, and R. H. Blyth, an Englishman, was invited to tutor the Crown Prince. Each was responsible for a major leap in the movement of haiku to the Western hemisphere. Blyth's four volumes of haiku (published between 1949 and 1952) contain hundreds of translated poems plus comments. These books were sold at foreign language bookstores throughout East Asia and in the United States.

In the late 1950's, Jack Kerouac's popular novel *The Dharma Bums* and Harold G. Henderson's *An Introduction to Haiku* arrived in American bookstores. Kerouac's book became a guide to a generation of American youth. In the opening fifty pages, the reader is introduced to Japhy Ryder, a character based on Gary Snyder. Japhy writes haiku and reads the complete works of D.T. Suzuki.

Teachers were discovering Henderson's *An Introduction to Haiku*, and although his translations had titles and end-rime, his versions were reasonably accurate. Despite these limitations, the book became quite popular. The combined effects of Kerouac's and Henderson's books started hundreds of Americans writing haiku. Other Beat poets included Allen Ginsberg and Gary Snyder.

The Haiku Society of America was founded in 1968 by Harold G. Henderson and Leroy Kanterman to promote the writing and appreciation of haiku in English, and continues its active promotion of haiku through regional meetings, publications, and a website.

The Resources section at the end of this chapter lists haiku magazines that are currently publishing contemporary English-language poets.

Haiku in Canada

Canadian poets started publishing haiku later than their counterparts in the United States. Leonard Cohen published poetry between the late 1950s and early 1960s. His haiku dedicated to Frank and Maria Scott is likely the first haiku by a leading Canadian poet.

Summer Haiku

Silence
and a deeper silence
when the crickets
hesitate

Patrick Lane's *A Line Crow, A Caftan Magpie* was the first collection of haiku to be published in Canada, or more correctly, an experimental blending of haiku and ghazal. Other early Canadian haiku poets included Claire Pratt and Rod Wilmott.

In 1969, Eric Amann's *The Wordless Poem* stirred interest in the study of Zen in haiku. The Haiku Society of Canada was founded in Toronto by Eric Amann, Betty Drevniok and George Swede in 1977. Today Haiku Canada holds annual conferences across the country, and publishes the *Haiku Canada Review* and individual broadsheets for practising poets.

Part 10: Haiku resources

Websites

Haiku Canada
    http://www.haikucanada.org/

Founded in 1977, Haiku Canada is a society of haiku poets and enthusiasts dedicated to: promoting the creation and appreciation of haiku and related forms (tanka, renga, senryu, sequences, haibun, and visual haiku) among its members and the public at large; and fostering association, friendship, communication and mutual support among haiku poets in Canada and abroad.

Haiku Society of America
http://www.hsa-haiku.org/   .

The Haiku Society of America is a not-for-profit organization founded in 1968 by Harold G. Henderson and Leroy Kanterman to promote the writing and appreciation of haiku in English. Membership is open to all readers, writers, and students of haiku. The HSA has been meeting regularly since its inception and sponsors open lectures, workshops, readings, and contests.

Vancouver Cherry Blossom Festival
    http://www.vcbf.ca

Each year the city of Vancouver, British Columbia, celebrates its thousands of cherry trees in full bloom in their city with the Vancouver Cherry Blossom Festival. The festival includes musical events, tree sightings, lectures, photography contests, art contests and an internationally renown and respected haiku invitational contest with a "youth division." Visit the website for more information regarding the history of haiku in Canada, teaching haiku, photo galleries, and past winners of the haiku contest.

Haiku Chronicles
    http://www.haikuchronicles.com/

Haiku Chronicles is a non-profit, free educational poetry podcast designed to provide a better understanding and appreciation of the art of haiku and its related forms including senryu, renku, tanka, haibun, haiga, and more. In these podcasts, poets Alan Pizzarelli and Donna Beaver discuss the origins and poetic principles of these poetic forms in the English language, featuring poems by the most prominent poets of the genre. Some of the podcasts include: crafting of haiku, baseball haiku, haiku and the Beat poets.

The Haiku Foundation
   http://www.haikufoundation.com

The Haiku Foundation includes a haiku bibliography with hundreds of articles, essays, and books on haiku or about haiku. Jim Kacian, founder.

Michael Dylan Welch's E-zine: Graceguts
   http://sites.google.com/site/graceguts/

A compendium of articles and poetry about haiku and related forms.

AHA Poetry
   http://www.ahapoetry.com/

This is Jane Reichhold's world of poetry that will make you say, "Ah ha!" to the many short form genres of poetry: haiku, tanka, and traditional renga rules. Many excellent articles found here.

Daily Haiku
   http://www.dailyhaiku.org

Daily Haiku is a print and daily online serial publication that publishes the work of Canadian and international haiku poets, blending contemporary, experimental, and traditional styles to explore the boundaries of English-language haiku. Through our *special features* section, we also aim to chronicle the diverse and ever-changing landscape of contemporary haiku-related forms. Patrick Pilarski and Nicole Pakan are the editors.

Angela Leuck's Blog: A Poet in the Garden
   http://acleuck.blogspot.com/

Haiku/Tanka poet Angela Leuck keeps a blog that centers on the Montréal Botanical Gardens and her visits there—sometimes alone, sometimes with other poets. Insights and conversations are recorded in haiku and tanka.

Curtis Dunlap's Blog: Tobacco Road Poet
   http://tobaccoroadpoet.blogspot.com

A haiku poet from North Carolina blogs about poetry, articles, book reviews, current news in the haiku community, haiku events and conferences, with links to the following organizations and journals for haiku and related forms:

- *3Lights Gallery of Haiku*

- *Acorn*

- *Aha Poetry*

- *Ambrosia*

- *Atlas Poetica*

- *Bashō's Road*

- *Bottle Rockets Press*

- *British Haiku Society*

- *Contemporary Haibun Online*

- *Crimson Bamboo*

- *Daily Haiga*

- *Daily Haiku*

- *Eucalypt (Australia)*

- *Haibun Today*

- *Haiga Online*

- *Haijinx*

- *Haiku Canada*

- *Haiku Northwest*
- *Haiku Society of America*
- *Haiku World*
- *Heavy Bear*
- *Issa's Untidy Hut*
- *Lilliput Review*
- *Lynx*
- *Mann Library's Daily Haiku*
- *Modern Haiku*
- *Moonset*
- *Red Moon Press*
- *Riverbed Haiku*
- *Roadrunner Haiku Journal*
- *Simply Haiku*
- *Sketchbook Press*
- *Tanka Central*
- *Tanka Society of America*
- *The Electric Poetry network*
- *The Heron's Nest*
- *Turtle Light Press*
- *Wild Goose Poetry Review*
- *Worldfield Haikai Pub*

A few good books on haiku

It is not possible to list all the wonderful collections of haiku and haiku related materials that have been published over the years. Here is a sampling of books that I have used in workshops, loaned to friends, and generally enjoyed over a cup of hot green tea:

HAIKU, 4 volumes, Robert Blyth, Hokuseido, 1949—1952)

The Classic Tradition of Haiku, An Anthology, Steven Carter, Stanford, 1991

Haiku in English, by Harold Henderson, Charles E. Tuttle, 1967

The Haiku Anthology, ed. Cor van den Heuvel, Norton, 1999

Haiku Moment, An Anthology of Contemporary North American Haiku, ed. Bruce Ross, Charles E. Tuttle, 1993

Haiku, Canadian Anthology, ed. Dorothy Howard and Andre Duhaime, Editions Asticou, 1985

Red Moon Anthology, ed. Jim Kacian & others, Red Moon Press 1996; annually

Carpe diem: Anthologie Canadienne de haïku / Canadian Anthology of Haiku. A new haiku anthology featuring 40 English-language and 40 French-language poets, ed. By Terry Ann Carter and Marco Fraticelli (English) and Francine Chicoine (French), Les Éditions David & Borealis Press, 2008

The Haiku Handbook — 25th Anniversary Edition: How to Write, Share, and Teach Haiku, by William J. Higginson with Penny Harter, Kodansha International, 2010

How to Haiku: A Writer's Guide to Haiku and Related Forms, by Bruce Ross Tuttle Publishing, 2002

Writing and Enjoying Haiku: A Hands-on Guide, by Jane Reichhold, Kodansha International, 2002

Haiku: A Poet's Guide, by Lee Gurga, Modern Haiku Press, 2003

Haiku: Asian Arts and Crafts for Creative Kids, by Patricia Donegan, Tuttle Publishing, 2003

Haiku: One Breath Poetry, by Naomi Beth Wakan, Stone Bridge Press, 1997

A few good books on senryu (haiku:you)

Japanese Life and Character in Senryu, by Robert H. Blyth, Hokuseido, 1969

Senryu, Japanese Satirical Verses, by Robeth H. Blyth, Hokuseido, 1949

Senryu: Poems of the People, ed. J.C. Brown, Charles E. Tuttle, 1991

Light Verse from the Floating World, by Makoto Ueda, Columbia, 1999

Haibun

Part 1: Definition of haibun

Now that you know something about writing haiku, it is time to take the next step. Combining prose and haiku results in a Japanese literary form called haibun. If a haiku is an insight into a moment of experience, a haibun is the story or narrative of how someone came to have that insight. A haibun tells the story about something that you saw or did or imagined. It is important to remember that the haiku that follows the narrative should illustrate the point of your prose, or extend the prose — it does not capsulate what has been written. In haibun, the reader is moved by the interrelationship between the prose writing and the haiku.

Part 2: Example of traditional Japanese travel haibun

The Hilltop Temple

Matsuo Bashō (from A Haiku Journey: Narrow Road to a Far Province)

In the domain of Yamagata is a hilltop temple called Ryushaku-ji. Built in 860 by the great abbot Jikaku, it is situated in a particularly pure and tranquil spot. Many people told us we ought to see it, so we retraced our steps from Obanazawa, though the temple was about seventeen miles away.

It was still light, so after taking lodgings at a pilgrims' hostel at the foot of the hill, we climbed up to the temple on the hilltop. The hill consisted of massive boulders, one upon the other, out of which grew luxuriant pines and cypresses of great age, and the ancient earth and rocks were green with velvety moss.

The doors of the lesser sanctuaries were closed and we heard not a single sound. But edging around the cliff and scrambling over the rocks, we finally said our prayers before the main Buddhist sanctum.

In the profound tranquility and beauty of the place, our hearts felt deeply purified.

In this hush profound,
Into the very rocks it seeps —
The cicada sound.

Part 3: Example of a contemporary travel haibun

31 October: Siem Reap

John Brandi

Sitting in one of the ruins yesterday—Bantaey Samre—I felt full tranquility of stone, silence, and cloud that Angkor Wat is capable of delivering. Silver grasses rustled with light under a perfect electric-blue sky. A few dragonflies rode the heat waves, and from over a stone wall, a breeze carried the laughter of village girls jumping rope. Out of the corner of my eye, a lone frangipani tree seemed to bend, drink from a pool, then lift again into the air to enjoy its solitude. Peering from my own solitude, I discovered a carved chariot wheel, the Dharma, turning in a maze of ornate designs above the temple doorway. Moments later, a blossom twirled to the pavement from the same doorway, rolled up to me, and gave a soft nod:

> old self, new
> self, still
> self.

Part 4: Haibun techniques

Some haibun tell stories or reflect upon memories. Consider the following haibun by Cor van den Heuvel, (reprinted with permission by the author) from his book *A Boy's Seasons: Haibun Memoirs* (Single Island Press). In his introduction Cor writes, "Haiku moments involve the senses: seeing, hearing, smelling, tasting, or touching. You don't have to be a haiku poet to have such moments. Any of us can have one if we see or hear something so vividly and clearly that we have a feeling of unity, or oneness, with *it*, and by extension with Nature itself. It may be something as simple as the sound of your dog lapping water from his bowl in the kitchen on a hot summer day or the sight of spring sunlight shining on some sheets blowing on the line."

Note to Teachers

After reading the haibun, have students begin writing their own sports stories from childhood, or even the events leading up to a tournament or victory game that they are playing in right now. If they do not personally participate in a sport, they might consider another athlete from the world of boxing, hockey, soccer, tennis. Consider the Olympic Games in Vancouver, British Columbia. Ask the students if they recall where they were during those games. Notice that Cor has more than one haiku at the close of his haibun. If students have several haiku that link to their stories, remind them to include them all.

Baseball Season

Cor van den Heuvel

Spring was baseball. The first sunlit breezes of March drew me to my mitt, which had lain all winter on a bookshelf in my bedroom, well oiled and tied tightly around a baseball lodged in its pocket. The sunlight and breezes—a mix of cool and warm air—sparkling and flowing among puddles, trees, and grasses, around patches of leftover snow, and along the wet sides of roads, made me want to play a game of catch, to swing my arm through the slow and easy, then gradually faster and faster, motions of throwing a baseball: to send the ball sailing through the air so it smacks firmly into someone else's glove, then see it whirling back towards me and feel and hear it land with a solid, socking sound into my own mitt.

> March thaw
> the sounds of a game of catch
> from the driveway

Something so simple—just the throwing of that round, hard ball back and forth, over and over again. It seemed as if I could go on forever in the warm sunlight of spring afternoons. Sometimes in the loose grip of that repeated motion, fantasies of games and triumphs to come later in the season might rise up against the backdrop of the clear blue sky, and I would feel my arm bearing down even harder to send the ball whistling into the distant glove. (Look at that curveball! Maybe I should be a pitcher.) But most of the time it was only a mindless repetition—the ball just going back and forth—thought was simply turned off. My body and my "self" disappeared into the pleasure of the continuing moment. There was a timelessness about it. Everything resolved into the joy of the movement, the motion that didn't go anywhere.

> the ball sky high
> as the crack of the bat
> reaches the outfield

Later, as the areas of dry ground increased in size and the last of the snow hid deep under hedges or behind the garage, out would come the bat and the solid sound of ash against horsehide would be added to our song of spring. Then would come the pick up games in a field almost surrounded by the still-cool woods—and once in a while I would swing away in just the right pulling motion and the bat would send the ball soaring high and far, flying way over the pine trees beyond left field.

a spring breeze
flutters the notice
for baseball tryouts

Baseball season would continue on into the long days of summer, too, and there would even be warm, or hot, afternoons when we'd get to play on a regulation diamond in the park and do the long, slow dance of a "real" baseball game—punctuated with the regular swift movements from the mound to the plate and the sudden flurries of action around the bases or in the outfield—on into the evening and right into dusk, until we could no longer see the ball and I'd walk home under the newly risen moon to a cold supper, which my mother would reheat for me.

at the plate
looking out from under my cap
at the world

the batter checks
the placement of his feet
"Strike One!"

the infield chatter
floats out to deep center
summer breeze

slow inning
the right fielder is playing
with a dog

light rain
the line drive knocks up dust
from the wet basepath

changing pitchers
the runner on first looks up
at a passing cloud

picking up my glove
from the shade in right field
its coolness

after the game
a full moon rises over
the left-field fence

Camping is an activity that brings us into nature. The following haibun by Jim Kacian reveals description (where he is camping) and insight into the solitariness of animals and human nature and how this experience makes him aware of the "order" of things, the interconnectedness of things, the "mud and shine" of his own being. Notice, too, how Jim has named the species around him: the Canada geese, the sandhill cranes, the lowland muskrat. He gives particular attention to vivid images: orange tents, bright coloured fiberglass craft, and the strong straight flights of the kingfisher. Remember, haibun is a story that brought you to haiku: prose, haiku and title are all connected.

Tell the story of a camping experience, a cottage vacation, or simply a walk down your favourite street. Record details in the narrative; extend, or "link and shift" with a haiku.

The Order of Stars

Jim Kacian

All summer long I share this river with the various migrant species that come to shelter and feed in its bounteous arms: Canada geese and sandhill cranes, upland beavers and lowland muskrat, fleet trout and wallowing carp; and, most seasonally, other human beings, as well. With them I exchange small talk about crops and crappies (small fish), great blues and boats, the weather and the World Series. For a few months the most notable objects on the water are bright coloured fiberglass craft powered by noisy engines churning through the steady clear currents. Along the shore, silver trailers with out-of state plates and mud-spattered pickups beside orange tents pop up in the flood plain. Smokey fires and loud talk ride the wind.

> calm evening
> the ball comes play-by-play
> across the water

When autumn appears, and the waters cool, first week days, then all days, find the water devoid of men. It is at this time, when the river and I are alone, that I am most able to come to my senses, become most truly human. It is not that I do not enjoy the company of my fellow men. But their presence illustrates to me what a man is, while in their absence, I am permitted to think on what a man can be, and to represent him well here among the wild and untutored, where there is no preference for things human. I am most able to shed the veneer of humanity and simply be, a human animal amongst these other animals, a presence amidst their presences.

It is now, when the river is barren, that I am most forcibly struck by the solitariness of wild animals. How rare it is to see animals in the company of a species not their own. Bears do not traffic with deer, beavers give the muskrats a wide berth, and chipmunks dart away at the approach of a hare. Only the birds are accepted: upon the waters, intermingled, I espy mallards keeping company with Canada geese; the cranes and herons share the shingled bank; and the strong straight flights of the kingfisher are looped together by the barn swallow's arabesques.

The dog is happy enough on his own, quite apart from these deliberations. He races about for sheer joy, biting at the white water of the rapids, crackling leaves in haste to get from here to there for no purpose other than to do it.

> cloudless sky
> enjoying the dog
> enjoying the river

Settling down for the evening on a mossy spot along the bank I am calmed by the river's steady flow. The water which I had passed over making my way here during the day now passes me by, baring with it the traces of the many soils and landscapes it drains: Blue Ridge escarpment, Shenandoah Valley effluvium, Piedmont loess, mingle in these waters are the mud and shine of its passing. Also flowing, the shine of the bright moon, the dim halo of stars about it, and, in the dark woods, my own shining being —

> camping alone
> the crackle of small sticks
> in the fire

The next few haibun are written by Canadian haiku/tanka/haibun poet, Mike Montreuil. His "style" is a shorter prose piece, setting the mood for the haiku. Mike finds inspiration from his family and finds the humourous side of family outings. Take a good look at your own family: consider your siblings, your parents, your grandparents. Find a funny story to tell. Link and shift to a haiku.

Change

Mike Montreuil

After two months of hearing complaints from my nineteen-year-old daughter, I finally heard a *good morning* and *bye* when I left to work. It was another reason to scratch my head and wonder why her mood suddenly changed.

> a tease from her brother
> she snaps a response —
> love is in the air

Apollo

Mike Montreuil

If you could only see us, standing beside the enormous first stage engines of the Saturn rocket. The craft is huge and dwarfs everyone in the presentation hall at the Kennedy Space Center. Some argue that it is the most complicated flying machine ever built by man. To many of us growing in its era, Apollo was the triumph against all the conflicts that ailed our world. My wife takes a few more pictures of the Lunar Rover. I ask my fourteen-year-old son what he thinks. There is no answer…

> hip-hop in his ears
> my son eyes a girl —
> Houston we have a problem

Family

Mike Montreuil

I'm walking down the fourth floor hallway of this middle-aged Holiday Inn. My room with the sagging double beds is at the other end, now home to half of my son's hockey team. This year, poker has replaced the PS/2 for evening entertainment. Bill, our head coach, is at his doorway sipping single malt scotch. Like me, he wonders if the boys will obey his curfew. I doubt it too.

They're fifteen and full of galloping hormones. But, they do get along. I grab a beer from someone's cooler and watch the euchre game being played by four of the parents.

> Saturday evening —
> A last away tournament
> with my second family

The award winning American haiku and haibun poet, Roberta Beary, often writes about matters of the heart. In her first example, Roberta is playing with an "idea" within her title, which connects to the punctuation in her prose. Notice how a sense of order is established by the use of semicolons to list the exit lines, any one of which points to a loss of control for the person on the receiving end. Later she shifts to the translations of a storyline in a foreign film in her haiku. How do all these "complications" get worked out? Love is never easy! Find inspiration in Roberta's style to write a haibun concerning new love, a break up, or unrequited love.

The Proper Use of Semicolons

Roberta Beary

We both know it's over but I'm the first one to say it; no matter what I do it's never enough; I just want someone who isn't crazy; I'm not blaming anyone here; it's too complicated; I need to simplify my life; I met someone else but that's not why; it's possible to love someone but not be in love; it's over.

> heatwave—
> we pick the one
> with subtitles

In her next haibun Roberta uses unconventional punctuation (no capital letters, no end punctuation) and sentence structure, perhaps to add to the rebellion of the persona she is using in the haibun. She describes the linked haiku in this way, "Imagine that you met 'the one' in high school and let that person somehow slip out of your life. Would you be haunted by a recurring image of what might have been? This is the setting for "barfly." What feelings do I hope to evoke in the haiku? In illustrating the ceiling fan's slow twirl I want to underscore the sense of monotony in a bar scene and its regulars. The tip jar represents another level of the mundane. Juxtapose these images with the adrenaline rush of being with 'a bad boy the nuns warn you about' whose kisses 'just ooze out of you.' The haiku also serves to pinpoint the dreariness of the present atmosphere in the bar as contrasted with the more exciting past as viewed through the distorted lens of a barfly. Other nuances are also present. The swirl of the fan is like the ticking of a clock. Is it one long night of drinking or many? Is it a momentary longing for an old love or a regret that always is present? The answers depend on the reader. Think of it this way: The haiku serves to color the prose of the haibun. The final touch is what the reader's own experience brings to the interpretation."

barfly

Roberta Beary

i was just a kid in those days and he was one of the bad boys the nuns warn you about and my old man told me stay far away from that one but i couldn't help myself and when i saw him he was walking up to me with his marlboros tucked under his tee-shirt like marlon brando with those biceps and his hair smelled of his last smoke and he kissed me one of those long kisses that just ooze out of you and shake up your insides at the same time but what did i know back then not enough

which is why he'll always be the one that got away

last call
a ceiling fan stirs
the tip jar

Haibun can also appear as a sequence, a number of haibun united by some kind of theme. After reading the sequence, you will see that there is a description or manifestation of a photo in each piece; sometimes it appears in the prose, sometimes it appears in the haiku. The linked haiku are extensions of the stories told in the prose. For your own creative response to writing a haibun sequence, find a central image, which will serve as a key; then tell a story. Consider: water (in all its forms), fire, hands.

Photos: A Haibun Sequence

Terry Ann Carter

In his junior year, William K. James played football for the Lower Merion Aces, the toughest high school team in eastern Pennsylvania. We had yet to witness the slaughter in Dallas, hugging our new Dylan LP's close to our chests, never missing a Friday afternoon practice, never missing a game on Saturday morning. Through most of October, the cars lined up in the parking lot outside General (Hap) Arnold Field, three hours before kick off. Old Mr. Donaldson from the neighbourhood bakery sold hotdogs; crepe paper from car antennas floated in the autumn air; corsages of purple and white mums bounced up and down on the chests of proud mothers. Leaves piled under swings for excellent jumping off places.

> star quarterback
> his photograph
> in every girl's locker

By his senior year, William K. James had become a legend. His worship of the game was intensified by his knowledge of college football and Heisman Trophy winners. Jim Thorpe, Jim Brown, Roger Staubach—all names he reckoned with. Travelling by bus down to South Bend, Indiana, he watched the Fighting Irish play at Notre Dame.

> even grey skies
> cannot dim this light
> the drum major first on the field

Big competition came from Radnor High School. Pep rallies started Friday afternoon after period four with three thousand teenagers steaming into a gymnasium to sing *give peace a chance* and thump their hands against the polished wooden floor. The coaches called out names and the boys filed in one by one; we were a screaming tide of hormonal hysteria.

> school entrance
> blue cornflowers
> all along the bricked path

After his best game of the season, William's photograph appeared in the local paper. Readers all along the Main Line and parts of Philadelphia could see the bright eyed boy behind the fallen face guard and meditate on his statistics: 25 completions, 300 passing yards, 4 touchdowns with 0 interceptions—could read about his uncanny ability to read defensive formations.

> game day
> up and down the streets
> the honking horns

Senior prom unfolded like a gilded lily at the Upper Darby gold and Country Club. William K. James and his date, Sheila Stewart, were elected prom king and queen. They exchanged prom keys and had their pictures taken under an arch of artificial white roses. After all night dancing to *do wah diddy diddy* and *I want to hold your hand* and *rag doll* and *baby love*, we slumped into seats at the early morning diner to pour rum into orange juice.

> prom dress
> cut on the bias
> summer lightning

After graduation, William K. James followed in the wake of his hero, Roger Staubach, and enlisted for a tour of duty in Southeast Asia. Nightly, we turned on our television sets to watch a civil war within a civil war. South Vietnamese military operations, Buddhist protests, civil servants and dock workers in the port of Danang wreaking havoc in a chaotic coup against local government. Prime Minister Nguyen Cao Ky and General Westmoreland issuing incendiaries to torch an entire country.

> next to high fidelity
> war
> in our living rooms

In his letters home William wrote about the heat, the heaviness of flak jackets, spiders the size of cigarette cartons. He described the sounds of chopper fire, jungle rain, the upturned faces of peasant children, the limbless victims of war that would crawl like crabs across the tiles of open market places. He prayed the Hail Mary now for survival instead of football passes, his athletic body pumped to carry AR16's and magazines of extra ammunition. Unlike Roger Staubach, Naval commander, William K. James joined the Army. Unlike Roger Staubach, William K. James did not come home.

>   class reunion
>   photographs of the dead students
>   draped in black

Part 5: Articles of inspiration for teachers and students

Haibun: Union of Prose and Poetry (John Dunphy)

How I Write Haibun (Jeffrey Winke)

Haibun: Union of Prose and Poetry

John Dunphy

Some authors write prose, while others write poetry. A few try to distinguish themselves in both fields, with varying degrees of success. As a haiku poet, I have the option of writing works that combine prose and poetry in one unique form.

Haibun (pronounced 'hai-boon') is a haiku-related literary genre that consists of taut prose accompanied by one or more haiku. When written well, a haibun delivers the power and insight found only in the best prose and poetry.

The subject matter of a haibun can be drawn from one's personal experiences.

Battered Customers

My bookshop's original location was two doors away from a shelter for battered women. To ensure the security of its temporary residents, no sign identified the building. Of course, I was always painfully aware of its existence.

Many times I saw women, frequently accompanied by their children, emerge from cabs or police cars and enter the building. Occasionally the women carried a suitcase. More often, she and her children had only the clothes on their backs.

When these women learned that my book shop was a safe place and that I would never betray their whereabouts, they stopped by to browse and temporarily forget the misery that forced them to seek refuge at the shelter. Even after so many years, I still recall particular customers.

> *on reading a joke book*
> *her bruised face*
> *tries to smile*

The prose in a haibun is terse. The use of strong, carefully selected nouns and verbs should minimize the need for adjectives and adverbs. Think Hemingway at his best.

Off-White Supremacists

The Ku Klux Klan has held several cross burnings in my community. I observed one from a safe distance. About 150 figures in pointed hoods and long robes were gathered around a huge wooden cross that had been set aflame. A speaker harangued the crowd. A wind came up, and the brilliant robes rippled and shined at first, but grew duller as the rally went on, sullied by the oily smoke.

> *sunrise*
> *a cardinal perches on*
> *the charred cross*

The haiku following the prose should provide a powerful denouement that leaves no loose ends. When writing this haiku, there are two important maxims to keep in mind: The haiku should never be a mere reiteration of some point made in the prose, and it should be able to stand on its own as a literary work.

While personal experience surely provides the most riveting material for a haibun, its subject matter can also be derived from an incident one has learned about.

Last Day of Deer Season

I know a woman who has recently taken up hunting. Last autumn she went deer hunting with her father and a few of his buddies. They sat behind some brush near a deer trail for a considerable time but saw no prey. Suddenly, they heard dogs barking and decided to investigate.

A dog pack had surrounded a young doe. The animal bore a shotgun wound just above its left front leg. The woman's father estimated the wound was two days old. Its eyes were glazed over with pain.

My friend's father chased away the dogs, and the doe took refuge behind nearby brush. The hunting party encircled its hiding place and flushed it from cover.

Her father took careful aim at the animal's spine and squeezed the trigger. The doe dropped, gasped three times and died. He quickly dressed the animal, removing even its liver and heart for future meals.

It was getting late, and the hunters were about to leave in their vehicles when one of the men spotted a buck some distance away. He didn't have a clear shot in the fading light but, disappointed that he had bagged nothing, decided to risk it.

The buck ran into the woods. When the hunters examined the spot where it had stood, they found fresh blood. Since encroaching darkness made tracking the buck impossible, the hunters returned to their vehicles for the journey home.

> *dusk*
> *snarling dogs surround*
> *a wounded deer*

Some incidents are so poignant that the haibun virtually writes itself, as was the case with the following selection. The prose is like a highway leading to a destination that is the haiku.

Battlefield Memento

I recently learned of a Vietnam veteran whose battalion was overrun during a battle in the Ia Drang Valley. His company suffered a casualty rate of over 90 per cent during a 24-hour period of hand-to-hand fighting.

In the early 1990s this man and a few other Ia Drang veterans returned to Vietnam and walked that long-ago battlefield. He wanted to find some memento of that conflict, such as shrapnel or a shell casing, to leave beside that panel of the Vietnam Veterans Memorial—"The Wall"—that contains the names of his comrades killed during that battle.

But he found no war relics. Over the years nature had effaced all traces of that horrendous engagement. Beautiful flowers now bloomed where once men had died. Still, this veteran wanted some memento to lay at The Wall panel listing his fallen comrades.

> *next to names of war dead*
> *pressed flowers*
> *from their last battlefield*

Many haiku journals publish haibun, while some websites are devoted exclusively to this fascinating genre. The world of haibun awaits your exploration. With this essay as a passport, you are ready to begin your journey.

Notes

All haibun in this essay were written by the author and have been previously published. For an introduction to haiku, see his earlier essay for this blog at: http://www.stltoday.com/blogzone/book-blog/book-blog/2008/07/what-is-a-haiku-and-what-isnt/

How I Write Haibun

Jeffrey Winke

I've been staring at the title of this essay for some time with the dang cursor blinking on the screen of my laptop. The cursor seems to be taunting me, saying, "You don't know what to write, do you? You're a fancy-pants expert and can't figure out how to explain how you do what you do! How long are you going to sit there watching me blink, you phony doofus!"

I'll tell you… that @#!%& cursor is lucky I don't have a hammer nearby.

Luckily, writing haibun comes easier than writing a piece to tell others how it's done. Writing haibun can be easy for you as well. I have three approaches to writing haibun, which may inspire you to give it a try.

To me haibun offer a creative way to:

- Document a current experience
- Talk about something from my past
- Spin a tall tale

I think of haibun as being very short stories—flash fiction—that are punctuated by a haiku. With my haibun, the haiku reflect the same feel or tone of the story. It never summarizes or repeats the story. Also, the haiku needs to be good enough to stand on its own.

My approach is different from the old Japanese masters and many writing haibun today who base their haibun in nature. My haibun are based on the most complex animal living today: humans, thus they are based on human nature.

Right now, I'm sitting in a coffee shop with a couple dozen other people. To me, there's potentially that many haibun that could be written using each of them as the "stars of the stories."

For example, there's a guy here that caught my attention immediately. He's got a white bandage running the length of the bridge of his nose. My first thought is that he probably had something removed like sun blemishes, moles, or even an ugly wart. Or maybe his nose was broken and the bandage is really a splint to keep his honker straight while it heals.

Could he have literally walked into a door or been reaching for a blanket on the top shelf of a bedroom closet when a heavy, old leather diary bonked his schnauze. Whose diary and how did it get there?

Or maybe, just maybe he's really an alien and somehow part of his synthetic flesh got damaged and the bruises are fluorescent pink and green, so until it heals, it's better to keep it covered up and drink lots of coffee, because coffee helps it heal. And maybe he bruised his nose walking into a door or reaching for a blanket…. you can see where I'm going.

I could have fun writing a haibun story from the alien's perspective. He could be angry with himself for being so clumsy or he could be angry that someone carelessly put a book on top of a folded blanket stowed on a high shelf. Or maybe he's frustrated with the alien physician who is out of town until next Tuesday vacationing at an intergalactic resort.

Whichever direction I take, I'll write the story from beginning to end. Then, sometime later, I'll go back and clean it up. That's something I learned along the way. I'll write a haibun or a haiku and let it sit for a day or longer and it's like all the flaws and extra wording pops out after a little time, so it's easier to go back and clean it up.

So, you can see that one way I write haibun is from observation of people around me. You can tell from the example that any haibun I write about the bandaged nose guy will likely be a tall tale.

Back to the coffee shop, there's a couple of young women a few tables away from me. I have a good view of the face of one of them. She has a cute face but what captures attention is how animated her face is when talking to her friend. She's got enough expression in her face that you'd be captivated listening to her talk about how she got a parking ticket or got caught in a public restroom with the last three squares on the toilet paper spool. She clearly has the range of expression in her face that would make a drama teacher yelp for joy.

I could write a haibun about me observing her and wondering if she's telling her friend about a new boyfriend or moving into a new apartment or getting a new job or something uniquely spectacular. I bet if I listened hard — maybe leaned in or moved closer — with my eavesdropping I'd learn what the real topic is. The contrast of my imagined story with the real — probably pretty mundane — story could make for a dramatic documentation of a real experience. This type of haibun would fall into the documenting a current experience.

As far as a haibun based on something from my past, I did notice a young man sit down in the coffee shop with two young women. One of them appears to be his girlfriend and the other a mutual friend. Seeing the three of them brought back a memory of a really stupid experience I had in high school.

I had planned a party for an upcoming Saturday night, which was held in the basement of my family home. The stupid thing that happened was that I kind of invited two girls that I was dating at the same time to the party. I imagined that they would hang out on opposite ends of the room with friends and that I could casually drift between the two girlfriends.

It made incredible sense and I was convinced that it'd work. The night of the party, things were working as I imagined, until one of my girlfriends led me to a spot in the room where she surprised me with a long passionate kiss. I was thinking, "Wow — this is unexpected, but kind of nice." Of course, her PDA was timed right when the other girlfriend was coming down the stairs from visiting the first floor bathroom and of course in her line of view. For me, things deteriorated quickly. I had started the night thinking I was quite the player, and it ended with both girls dumping me. I had hurt them both with my selfish deception.

I've often thought there may be a haibun in that experience. I'm not sure I want to admit to being that heartless, so let's all agree that it was some other nameless jerk, not me. The haibun will be written in the third person about some other kid, rather than me confessing.

So, hopefully you have an idea of how I write haibun. The key thing I do is observe or think about experiences from my past, and then unleash my imagination. My goal is to create a fun story written in common, conversational language, and top it with a powerful haiku that reflects the feel or tone of the story.

You can do it too. Relax. Write like a mad person. Write a story or scenario from the start to the end without doubt or censoring. Write bunches of haiku the same way. Some haiku will be good. Some will never be good, but that's fine.

With the raw first draft of your haibun, you can go back and trim out the extra words, rewrite clumsy sentences, and add the sparkle and missing oomph. I replace lifeless verbs with all-out action words and add adjectives to flesh out the details that I see in my head. I make sure that there are no extra words in my haiku.

To summarize... I write haibun based on human nature—what I see, feel, and hear while living my life in a modest-sized city. I document my experience that occurs now or in the past. And I let my imagination enhance or create scenes that can be real or totally fictional. I also write recklessly from beginning to end, but then go back—sometimes multiple times—to clean, prune, and spruce up what I've written.

My approach works for me. It may work for you or help you discover your own approach to writing haibun or getting more enjoyment out of reading them.

Part 6: Haibun resources

Narrow Road to the Deep North, by Matsuo Bashō, translated by Nobuyuki Yuasa, Penguin Books, 1966

The Spring of My Life, by Issa, Sam Hamill, Shambala Press, 1997

Japanese Poetic Diaries, ed. Earl Miner, University of California, 1969

Journey to the Interior: American Versions of Haibun, by Bruce Ross, Charles E. Tuttle, 1998

Tanka

Part 1: Definition of tanka

In *The Haiku Handbook: How to Write, Share, and Teach Haiku*, William J. Higginson devotes an entire chapter to tanka that he calls "Before Haiku." Tanka, was in fact, an older poetic form, or song, dating back to the Nara through Heian Periods in Japan. Here you will find a history of this poetic form with accounts of Shiki, Mokichi, and Yosano Akiko. Tanka is a highly personal and emotional poetry; in Japanese, it is written in five lines or phrases in a pattern of 5-7-5-7-7 syllables. Kozue Uzawa, editor of Gusts: Contemporary Tanka, explains that English tanka should come closer to 20 syllables. She invites us to write directly and express our feelings freely.

Part 2: Examples of Japanese traditional tanka

My longing for you —
too strong to keep
At least no one can blame me
when I go to you at night
along the road of dreams

Ono no Komachi

No different, really —
a summer moth's
visible burning
and this body
transformed by love

Lady Izumi Shikibu

Part 3: Examples of contemporary tanka

In the poet's words: "In order to live sanely, there is no alternative to a positive, compassionate and cheerful willingness to simplify and strongly keep going forward as best we can. The troubles in one's personal life and those of the world constantly threaten the balance we try to maintain. Difficulties occur at any stage in life, but tanka has been an invaluable tool for me in finding my way through turn after turn."

Tom Clausen, American tanka poet

feels like
there's a cliff
in my head
crumbling
day by day

Takuboku

the cold walk,
silence
between us,
the creek running
under ice

Tom Clausen

the tentative start up
of talk...
  to a new friend?
begins the old doubt
of just who I am, again

Tom Clausen

I've this memory —
  riding my father's shoulders
  into the ocean,
  the poetry of things
  before I could speak

        Michael McClintock

her china cup
on the floor
in pieces —
so how do you mend
a broken heart?

        Lois Harvey

I know
you're the woman for me —
when I give you flowers
you keep them in a vase
until they're totally dead

        Owen Bullock

I'm showing off again
in front of
a female —
will these urges
ever fail?

        Owen Bullock

spin the bottle
nobody
wants to kiss
the girl
with pimples

        Pamela Babusci

peer pressured
to have sex
she stands confused
outside
the clinic

Pamela Babusci

outside the church
falling petals
of the weeping cherry
another
teen suicide

Pamela Babusci

benched
the star forward
his sweat
and the clock ticking
down

Barry George

for me
it's the slow, graceful
high arcing
from the corner
jump shot

Barry George

four years on this street
and today I see the fire hydrant
as if for the first time
what else have I walked by
and not really seen

Philomene Kocher

high school reunion
yes, after fifty years
each of us
has become
what we were

Guy Simser

I catch the first bus
heading East—
all across Canada
mile after mile
of leaving him

Angela Leuck

that old crow
pecking away at a piece
of dried husk...
how painful this parting
with hearts still soft

Carole MacRury

4 am
whispers
in my ear...
another phone-in
on loneliness

Helen Buckingham

crowds exit
the trashed
stadium—
turning on the tv
somebody claims to have won

Helen Buckingham

rain washes the dust
from the bus window
and I can see
more clearly
what tears do

Philomene Kocher

no longer a child
the first time
I tied my own skates too tight
setting a pattern
to unbind decades later

Philomene Kocher

on the gull's beak
a blood-red spot
my guilt
so long concealed
has become nameless

Carole MacRury

Sometimes a number of tanka can be written on one topic (not to be confused, however, with a tanka sequence). The sequence is narrative. Here are examples of both: "Five Moon Tanka" are simply tanka written about the moon. "And, Sometimes In Me" is a tanka sequence written when I returned home from a teaching experience in China.

Five Moon Tanka

Terry Ann Carter

haze around
the morning moon
Auschwitz survivor
shows his tattoo
to the grade ten class

how often
I go to the window
watching for his car
the lonely moon
at the end of the street

the Slavic grandmother
of my friend
wears her babushka
like a crescent moon
around her chin

abalone moon
whispered secrets
of the disappeared women
their graves, not far
from the sea

dinner party
the men talk hockey
the women talk babies
that old moon finds its place
in the sky

And, Sometimes In Me: Tanka Sequence

Terry Ann Carter

Home from China
each rounded leaf
reminds me of moon gates
this summer night
fanning against my skin

Where can I find
a bamboo bird cage
like those in Shanghai markets
the slow scuttle
of clouds

Finally finding
my bamboo cage
in an antique shop
the owner wearing
new red shoes

Nothing lives
in the wooden cage
only a memory
of a creature
who sang before dawn

And, sometimes in me,
a great desire
to lift open
the little door
let something fly free

Part 4: Articles of inspiration for teachers and students

From the Beginning: Introducing Students and Teachers to the Grand Master of Tanka in the Western World—Sanford Goldstein (Terry Ann Carter)

Notes on Form, Techniques, and Subject Matter in Modern English Tanka (Michael McClintock)

Tanka for Teens (Amelia Fielden)

Notes from an English Teacher Tackling Tanka (Dorothy Maloney)

The Poetry of Things Before I Could Speak: A Very Short Pedagogical Thought for Teachers Who Juggle Forty Balls in the Air at One Time (Terry Ann Carter)

From the Beginning: Introducing Students and Teachers to the Grand Master of Tanka in the Western World— Sanford Goldstein

Terry Ann Carter

Sanford Goldstein has been on the "tanka road" for more than forty years. He is recognized as the grand old man of tanka and is loved and appreciated around the world for his writing, his mentorship and friendship, his translations and collaborations. He has been a judge for international contests and has edited several anthologies, most notably, *Sixty Sunflowers* from the Tanka Society of America Members' Anthology for 2006-2007. As well as his translations of classic modern Japanese poetry, he has written some of the best tanka ever rendered first in English. Six published collections are compiled in his historic volume, *Four Decades on My Tanka Road*. Among the books he has co-translated with Professor Seishi Shinoda are *Songs From a Bamboo Village*, and *Tangled Hair*.

Sanford Goldstein taught literature and creative writing in the United States (Professor Emeritus at Purdue University) and continued his professorship, after retirement, at Keiwa College, in Japan. He has resided in Japan for the last 18 years and has been studying Japanese for more than 54 years. He is still trying to improve his hearing and speaking of the language, and often says that he wouldn't be able to translate without the assistance of his Japanese partners.

Many of Sanford's poems are short reflections on his own childhood, on education, marriage, retirement, old age and illness. Whether the poems are from a personal point of view, or an impersonal perspective, they frequently use images from nature. Sanford is also inspired by his love of literature, theatre, dance and art. He attempts to touch the extreme limits of his life with a language that carries simplicity, warmth, humour, and emotion. Here are excerpts from his "Biography" from *Four Decades on My Tanka Road*, of course, written in tanka:

Biography

my mother:

at times, Mother,
with your peripheral vision
you called me by some other name
as if you wanted
twice the love

my wife:

rest
dear wife
from no-thought
from riddles of the universe
from the master's command

my children:

thick donuts
in a brown bag:
a kid offering
to this Sunday
god of wrath

my friend:

at the end
of my white string
a soulmate came,
so close to the edge
I could not scissor it away

my teaching:

for fifty four years
long comments on student
compositions –
yours, Thomas Wolfe,
longer, more passionate

my spanned life:

I have used sandpaper
to smooth down
the rough edges of
forty years of pain –
I'm a gloss, I'm a précis

With his translating partner, Seishi Shinoda, Sanford has been responsible for translating numerous works of modern Japanese literature into English. In addition to the books available through major publishers, there are several collections of his own poetry available through small literary presses. Sanford makes himself available to assist young poets and teachers wishing to learn more about the world's oldest continually anthologized poetic genre—tanka.

You may reach him at goldsteinsanford@yahoo.com.

Note To Teachers

Looking at "Biography" as a model for tanka writing, have students consider their own lives, particularly relating to relationships, and compose a series of tanka. The final poem could be a summation of a life lived for fifteen (or specific number of) years. Turn students' attention to the last lines "I'm a gloss, I'm a précis." Which words work preferably for your students?

Acknowledgment

I wish to thank Patricia Prime, co-editor of New Zealand's haiku magazine *Kokaku,* for her notes on Sanford and her warm encouragement. More detailed information may be found in her "An Interview With Sanford Goldstein Parts I, II, III" in the Tanka Society of America's online archive.

Notes on Form, Techniques, and Subject Matter in Modern English Tanka

Michael McClintock

In form, techniques, and subject matter, the modern English-language tanka shows wide variation and invention, and appears disinclined to observe any rigid set of "rules" or conventions.

As might be expected in the early stages of adaptation, English-language tanka poets first imitated the Japanese models and strictly adhered to a 5-7-5-7-7 syllabic structure and pattern of short/long/short/long/long lines deduced from them. Generally, this resulted in poems that were too long in comparison to Japanese tanka or that were padded or chopped to meet the fixed number of syllables. Over time, most tanka poets set aside the 5-7-5-7-7 requirement and explored a more resilient free-verse approach, grappling along the way with the issues of using or not using rhyme, titles, and alternate lineation schemes. The work of the leading translators was assiduously studied. Most of these, such as Makoto Ueda, Stephen D. Carter, Sanford Goldstein, and Laurel Rasplica Rodd rendered their translations in five lines. There were other approaches, however. H. H. Honda advocated the use of the quatrain for tanka; Kenneth Rexroth occasionally used a four-line structure in his renderings of Japanese tanka. Hiroaki Sato continues to favor the one-line format for his translations.

While poets continue to experiment, the contemporary tanka in English may be described as typically an untitled free-verse short poem having anywhere from about twelve to thirty-one syllables arranged in words and phrases over five lines, crafted to stand alone as a unitary, aesthetic whole—a complete poem. Excepting those written in a minimalist style, a tanka is about two breaths in length when read aloud. During the last thirty years, it has emerged as a robust short form that is identifiable as a distinct verse type while being extremely variable in its details.

Other structural features and many of the techniques and subjects of English-language tanka are represented in the examples discussed below.

For every tanka set aside here for scrutiny, ten others might have been chosen to serve the same purpose. Within the five lines, all manner of variation takes place. None of these configurations is rigidly observed; the name I have used for each is meant only to describe the structure and lineation.

Few tanka poets write consistently in a single, unvaried pattern of line arrangement. The alternation of short and long lines frequently varies. While the majority of tanka in English appear with a left-aligned or "flush left" margin, many poets employ indentations, staggered lines, and other spacing variations. These arrangements emphasize certain lines, phrases, or single words, or give the poem a sense of movement or shape on the page that is intended to enhance the meaning, tone, or emotion evoked. A few variations appear simply to be matters of the poet's (or editor's) own taste, or purely cosmetic, such as the centering of lines the example below:

[Centered, 5-7-5-7-7 formal pattern]

Just out of earshot,
the periodic blinking
of a night airplane,
not quite far enough away
to be as close as the stars

Gerald St. Maur

Other fundamental elements of structure are also at work, creating tension and interplay of form with content. These have to do with cadence, rhythm, accents, or stresses, the use of end-stopped lines or rhetorical line breaks, caesuras within lines and phrases, enjambment, juxtaposition of images, or a pairing of distinct strophe-antistrophe components within the poem. These elements—not the number of syllables in a line—are the decisive elements in tanka structure as written in English. In contrast to Japanese tanka, which mostly use a fixed, prescribed form with a long history of formal conventions relating to mechanics, techniques, and subject matter, tanka in English have relatively few such constraints or requirements in pattern or organization. In English-language tanka, we find intuitive, functional, and organic approaches to form and content that result in a complex but necessary interrelationship of parts; no bodies of "rules" need to be followed to achieve the desired effect of the whole. While informal syntax and the patterns and vocabulary of common speech predominate, these very broad commonalities display remarkable, polychromatic diversity in tone, mood, and expression.

As with many tanka in this set of examples, this poem by Ruby Spriggs reflects traditional tanka subject matter, involving topics of love, sorrow, personal remembrance or introspection, or nature:

[Conventional flush left, 5-7-5-7-7 formal pattern]

a sudden loud noise
all the pigeons of Venice
at once fill the sky
that is how it felt when your hand
accidentally touched mine

Ruby Spriggs

Often, tanka read like notes from a diary and convey a single event that has some special significance in the poet's life or consciousness—a realization, personal insight, or memory. Spriggs's poem also shows how the basic structural features of Japanese tanka have been adapted. The pattern of short/long/short/long/long lines is intact, and the use of thirty-one syllables in five lines of 5-7-5-7-7 parallels the pattern of thirty-one sound units of Japanese tanka. This is one of the formal patterns tried by many poets for English-language tanka during the early days of experimentation and adaptation; some still use it today, and in the literature it is frequently referred to as "traditional." It results in a poem that is, however, almost twice as long in time duration as a Japanese tanka, with a good deal more information.

"Venice" won first prize in the traditional category in the First North American Tanka Contest held in 2001. The judge, Professor Jan Walls, author and oriental scholar at Simon Fraser University, commented on how the poem "takes the familiar touristic image of startled pigeons simultaneously taking flight, and unexpectedly relates the cause/effect sequence to a personal romantic incident. The imagery is fresh and startling; the content is powerfully meaningful . . . at the personal level; and the craft is exquisite—it reads like a tanka, but will be immediately appreciated by any English reader who may know nothing about tanka."

Here, Margaret Chula also uses the 5-7-5-7-7 formal pattern:

> the black negligee
> that I bought for your return
> hangs in my closet
>   day by day plums ripen
>   and are picked clean by birds

Margaret Chula

Both poems are dramatic and anecdotal, telling a story in few words but with intensity and conviction. However, here indentation is used to emphasize the poem's two component movements. Rather than a personal comment or reflection, Margaret Chula's final two lines offer a stark "objective correlative" to the image and mood of the preceding three lines, encapsulating the poet's thoughts in implicit metaphor. The juxtaposition is surprising, and the despairing realization is made even more powerful by not being named—the bleak image of the ripened plums "picked clean by birds" says it all. Unlike the Spriggs poem, the two images here are not directly compared but set in sharp contrast. The effect approaches, but is not quite, surreal.

William Ramsey's tanka illustrates a reversal in the basic two-component structure, the couplet element coming first and bearing the poem's single image:

> a gnat's smudge
> on my forearm —
> > the smallest death
> > i have known this year
> > but typical

William Ramsey

The poet's response in the final three lines is made more acerbic by "falling back" to a short, concluding line.

Consider also the movement in Geraldine Clinton Little's poem:

> ah, summer, summer,
> how quickly you fade. I cut
> > rusted zinnias,
> place them on a glassed table-
> > top, as if time could double.

Also a poem of 5-7-5-7-7 syllables, this tanka is more complicated, having three parts and given momentum by the use of enjambment: "ah summer, summer / how quickly you fade" functions as the strophe, "I cut / rusted zinnias, / place them on a table- / top," is the antistrophe, and the poem's sliding to a rest on "as if time could double" functions as a kind of epode. The enjambed strophes and abrupt shifts generate tension and underscore the poet's wistful contemplation of time's evanescence. The reflected double-image of the zinnias on the glass tabletop is an especially powerful image, again showing the use of an objective correlative to convey both idea and emotion while preserving aesthetic distance.

Carol Purington's poem, below, is distinctly lyrical.

> The days I did not sing
> > the nights I did not dance
> > > their joy
> > > > spiraling out of the throat
> > > > of a hermit thrush

The parallel construction of the opening two lines is that of a song. The strong accents on the final words in each line move the poem forward with a

130 LIGHTING THE GLOBAL LANTERN

sense of "lifting." The poem's progression from the general "The days I did not sing" to the specific and beautiful "throat of a hermit thrush" is lilting— almost like a bird in flight. The staggered line arrangement visually assists this sense of movement. If its lines were all aligned left, how different this poem would read!

In this poem by Gerald St. Maur, the first three lines could stand alone as a haiku, a feature that may be found in many contemporary English tanka:

Just out of earshot,
the periodic blinking
of a night airplane,
not quite far enough away
to be as close as the stars

Such tanka combine the objective imagery of a haiku with a subjective response or personal reflection in the poem's concluding lines; the order can also be reversed. It is the subjective element in a tanka that chiefly distinguishes it from most haiku, in addition to its greater length. Here, the concluding two-line component is a simple, personal reflection or response to the initial image, placing the silent aircraft in the context of a starry sky. The twist in sense here—that the aircraft is the more remote, alien object—gives a postmodern slant to the traditional tanka theme of loneliness.

A feature of many tanka in English is the employment of one of several conceptually related devices or methods that are used to change the direction of the tanka between the first and second components. This transition is often called the "pivot." Sometimes it is achieved simply by juxtaposing two images, or an image and a response, or by the movement from strophe to antistrophe. At other times the pivot functions like the volta, or turn, in a sonnet, where the sense of the poem is momentarily suspended and a new idea introduced—this is what occurs in the line "their joy" in Carol Purington's poem, and in the line "not quite far enough away" in Gerald St. Maur's tanka. Ruby Spriggs accomplishes her pivot with a hemistich or half line: "that is how I felt . . ." Sometimes, too, the pivot in a tanka is achieved by a line that completes the thought or image of the first component, or strophe, and can be read also as the first line of the second component, or antistrophe. In other words, the sense of the line is shared by both components, but changes in meaning or significance from one to the other. The term for this technique is "zeugma." Francine Porad is especially adept in using pivots of this kind. Here is an example, in which "as the train passes" is the shared line:

a woman
holds the waving child high
as the train passes
where . . . when . . .
did summer disappear

In such tanka, the strophe and antistrophe are the key units of composition. Some critics appear to think that the presence of a pivot in tanka is essential, taking the Duke Ellington view of rhythm and jazz: "It don't mean a thing if it ain't got that swing." Must all tanka have such a pivot point? Most tanka in English seem to, though it frequently can be so subtle as to go unnoticed. At other times, the pivot is emphatic and surprising. There is, in fact, no requirement for the use of this technique, in English-language or Japanese practice. Its absence does not mean the poem is not a tanka.

Robert Kusch writes a tanka in a more minimalist style:

Lightning on
the horizon
my child
takes a huge
bite from a pear

Kusch uses a syntactic pivot: two images are simply juxtaposed, or abutted, without transition or even punctuation. No subjective element or stated interpretation appears; we assume only a temporal contiguity between the two images. The immediacy and effect are very haiku-like and defy paraphrase or elaboration. Such force holds the combined images together so that they fuse into a third image that is stunning, magical, wordless, yet utterly mysterious in meaning or significance. The Japanese have a word for it, *yugen*, meaning sublimity, or mysterious depth.

Another minimalist poem is LeRoy Gorman's droll "at the funeral," a mere fourteen syllables:

at the funeral of
one who said
God is dead
God is
dead

The structure is Skeltonic, tumbling from six syllables to one, ending emphatically on the word "dead." It is one breath in length, like a haiku, a trait shared by most minimalist tanka. Unlike haiku, it contains no image. For these reasons, and because of its content, some might argue that the poem is more akin to senryu, haiku's satirical cousin. Many minimalist tanka present this same quandary of classification—would they not be haiku or senryu if written in the conventional three lines of those genres? It is not a problem that will be resolved here; like most minimalist poems, Gorman's poem seems to take an insurgent posture toward any comfortable definition. It represents a crossover tanka. Others who have used this technique include ai li, Fay Aoyagi, Sanford Goldstein, Philip Rowland, Alexis Rotella, and others. They are so numerous, in fact, that perhaps they represent a subgenre of tanka in English.

Many English-language tanka might in fact be regarded by most Japanese as being a subgenre of tanka, known as *kyoka*, or "mad poems," containing satire, sometimes even crudity, with little or no attempt to be lyrical. These poems are sometimes like an epigram, humorous and opinionated, occasionally acerbic and biting. At the other end of the spectrum, they may be playful or light in mood or, like Gorman's, gently mocking in tone. The kyoka is to the tanka what senryu is to the haiku. Like senryu, they can be rather sharp, penetrating observations of human faults, foibles, and failings. A confessional quality is present in those where the poet is both observer and observed.

Some of the finest English-language tankaists frequently write in kyoka style. Here is one by Laura Maffei:

energy waning
as the afternoon wears on
a grim coworker
leans into my cubicle
whispering conspiracy

Such comic portrayals of modern life, often containing social or political commentary, are very much the substance, voice, and character of tanka in English, and represent its departure from the traditional subject matter of Japanese tanka. Leatrice Lifshitz's encounter with a green pepper, below, is a further illustration:

I
  who am not really
    a cook
  poke gently into
    a green pepper

At present, there seems little practical reason to separate these seemingly kyoka-like poems and make them a subgenre, or to place them in a class by themselves and call them something else; they are too much a part of what tanka *is* in English. Values are based on inclusions as much as exclusions.

Anne McKay's tanka represents still another approach to structure, introducing the dimension of space:

centered
by north light
the potter's wheel
small dreams
within the curve of her hands

The words appear to float on the page, invested with light, eddying toward the final image of the potter's hands. This tanka is one of a series by mckay that deal with the subject of light, invoked as both physical phenomenon and metaphysical presence. The poem's form accords perfectly with its content and delicate lyricism.

In the foregoing examples, punctuation either is absent or kept to the bare minimum. This is typical of most tanka in English. Only a few poets — Alexis Rotella and Pamela Miller Ness are two — consistently use periods at the end of lineated sentences or at the end of a poem; they also use initial capitals. These features give their tanka a very slight, relative formality. Other poets, such as George Swede and Karina Young, capitalize only the first word of a tanka. Many have used different approaches over the years.

Metrical patterns, or accented metric feet, are certainly possible in the English-language tanka. Such patterns would be meaningless in Japanese, which places a uniform stress on the last syllable of each word. English syllables do not equate to the Japanese sound unit; converting English syllables to Japanese sound units, or vice versa, is not a one-for-one exchange. Some tanka in this collection do, in fact, show deliberate use of accentual meter in their lines, adding to the poem's other dimensions of rhythm, sound, and fluidity when read silently or aloud. In the following tanka by Cherie Hunter Day, the basic metric unit is the iambic foot, one short or unstressed syllable followed by a stressed or long syllable (lines one to four):

through patterned glass
see how the water bends
the flower stems
my heart and many other
optical illusions

The iambic rhythm breaks in the fifth line, where a dactyl foot (OP-ti-cal) is followed by an amphibrach foot (il-LU-sions), playfully emphasizing the sense and meaning of the words.

While set rhyme schemes have never been used in tanka, traditional end rhyme and internal rhyme do occasionally occur. Slant and half-rhyme, involving assonance and consonance, appear with greater frequency. These uses of rhyme work in conjunction with alliteration, caesura, and line breaks to emphasize certain words or phrases, to control the pace or cadence in a tanka, to build or release tension, and to help make one movement in a poem distinct from another. Assonance in the last two lines of this tanka by John Barlow conveys a subtle and unusual musicality:

> dawn
> and you open
> your deep-green eyes—
> blackbirds stir
> somewhere in the conifers

Almost all issues continue to be argued and debated by poets, scholars, and critics. James Kirkup in Andorra argues in favor of a strict adherence to a 5-7-5-7-7 syllabic measure in English. Gerald St. Maur has advocated the use of titles for individual tanka, while others argue that in a poem so brief this is tantamount to adding a sixth line. A compromise might be the occasional use of a simple head note; in Japan, a head note often appears with a tanka to provide information pertinent to the poem's composition, such as where it was written, on what occasion or event, or some other detail. However, these head notes do not function as titles do. Of course, titles are used for tanka collections, sequences or "strings," and other groupings.

While the method and craft of tanka in English varies considerably from the conventional rigors of Japanese practice, clearly both approaches result in verses that manifest and share similar poetic mood and temper. In each, the powers of compression, nuance, implication, and understatement are orchestrated to evoke emotion or describe an image or experience. Variations that do exist reflect differences in culture and language. We can speak of "the tanka spirit" as a quality in the poems that is held broadly in common, in much the same way as haiku poets throughout the world today speak of "the haiku spirit." The tanka of Japan appear to embody intrinsic values of expression and understanding that are robust enough to not only survive but also thrive when transferred to another culture and language.

It may be argued that the differences between Japanese tanka and its English-language counterpart are less important than the intrinsic similarities. They indeed have much in common, but beyond a certain undefined point—one that is perhaps intuited only—differences are certainly to be expected and even encouraged, so that each may take full advantage of the resources of its own language and culture. Tanka in English may deviate within the tanka tradition in order to create their own distinct flavor and build their own integrity, while at the same time preserving the formal and mechanical techniques that are fundamental to all tanka.

Tanka for Teens

Amelia Fielden

Tanka is a very ancient form of Japanese poetry, dating back over 1300 years. It is also a very modern form of expression for hundreds of thousands, from junior high school students to retired folk, living all over the world.

In the late nineteenth and early twentieth centuries, a group of young poets brought this classical poetry of Japan into the contemporary world through experimenting with new and innovative themes for their tanka. They, and the poets of today, have proved that even specifically modern ideas can be conveyed effectively through a traditional form.

Tanka composition thrives and maintains a mass market in contemporary Japan. Hundreds of books of tanka are published annually. Some of them, like *Salad Anniversary* by Tawara Machi, which sold almost 3 million copies in its first printing, are a huge success. Newspapers carry weekly tanka columns edited by well-known poets, who select for publication from among thousands of tanka submitted by a nation-wide readership. Regular tanka programs are shown on mainstream television channels. And so on.

Where do all these poets and lovers of tanka come from? Well, tanka writing and appreciation is taught to teenagers throughout Japan in their schools and colleges.

And for the past 23 years, Toyo University in Tokyo has held a major competition for tanka written by teens. In 2009, 63,000 entries from around the nation were received. Though love and romance were obviously on the minds of many of the teenaged authors, the subjects of the tanka later selected for publication in the book *One Hundred Tanka by Young Students Today* are extremely varied. Anything goes, as they say. Here are just a few of such tanka (translated into English):

> the length of time
> since I first met him
> is
> the length
> of my uncut hair

Yukari Chono, age 16

mesmerized
by the blue of the autumn sky,
I again fail to grasp
the teacher's words
in my Japanese class

Ayaka Euchi, age 15

my breath white,
I get out of the wheelchair
step on the ground
and feel the heat
of the Earth's core

Takahiro Nakano, age 16

people knew all too well
they were selling
contaminated rice —
which was more contaminated
the rice or their hearts?

Keisuki Goda, age 18

let's have
an Obama sensation
in Japan, too —
everyone is waiting for
a trustworthy prime minister

Kaori Matsumura, age 16

There are lots of books of tanka by young people — and there are tanka on mobile phones, too. A very popular way for young Japanese to connect with each other is by texting in tanka. How about trying that …

Notes from an English Teacher Tackling Tanka

Dorothy Maloney

My students worked intensively on a different tanka each day and submitted them to me as a ticket out the door. As a college level class they are not good at completion of tasks or deadlines but this assignment worked so well. Also it was easier to concentrate on something of five lines and really work on revision. They were quite pleased with their results.

I picked three words from each student's tanka (that I thought were not as strong as possible) and wrote them on separate sheets with no names. The students didn't know where the words came from at that moment. We passed the sheets around and they used a thesaurus or thought of a surprising word associated with that word. Then I returned the final tanka with the underlined words, and they looked at their poems and were encouraged to consider how the possibilities spun the tanka in new directions. We had previously worked on a clozed poem exercise with "The city of my heart." I asked them if they had achieved "tanka mastery" and their answers were interesting. It was some of their best writing.

We have been writing tanka in order to reach tanka mastery and in the process we have discovered how to generate ideas, experiment with forms and style, draft and revise, edit and proofread, provide feedback to peers, assess peers' work, study tanka masters, understand our creative choices, improve and demonstrate growth, creating a final product but also publishing a class chapbook. Later, some of the students wrote haiku (with sidewalk chalk) on the parking lot for Poetry Month in April.

An evaluation rubric I developed appears on the following page.

The Tanka Experience

Name:_____

The Curriculum expectations for EWC4C are organized into 3 strands:

Investigating writing

Practising Writing

Reflecting on Writing

Categories		E	G	S
Thinking — the use of critical and creative thinking skills and/or process, planning	Peer commenting Evaluating self Ability to improve tanka Word choice Drive to write more			
Knowledge — subject specific content and the understanding of its meaning and significance	Pivot line Big picture/little picture Impact of images Minimalist /Free form/ Syllable counts			
Communication — conveying of meaning through various forms, conventions- spelling, grammar, punctuation	Expression of idea Organization Form of the final tanka Spelling /Grammar Punctuation			
Application — the use of knowledge and skills to make connections	Connects concrete to abstract Growth from first tanka to final tanka Ability to go beyond five lines on the page Use of metaphor/ analogy Wow factor			

How many tanka did you attempt?

How did you improve your final tanka?

What should I consider about your writing process?

Tanka Mastery

Grade 12 Writers Craft

Essex District High School, Windsor, Ontario

I'm always counting
The weeks before I see you
How can I measure
Seconds as they pass each day
Time seems to stop without you

Jessica Pringle

It happens
In slow motion
One million things
Never to be said
I continue walking

Michael Nantais

Inspiring thoughts
Make my heart spill
Like a glass of water
Knocked over
By powerful words

Lauren Ferris

The great captain
Loves his boat
Sails it far and wide
But does not subside
The feeling he's hiding inside

Dylan McAllister

Colored leaves:
Orange, crimson, yellow, rust
Fall from the trees
I see this wind blow them
So far out of my reach

Amy Puhl

Today is the day
That the world will fall apart
It will happen so fast
so quickly
just crashing

Ryan Groves

I have walked this path before
Decaying trees all around me
Blackened soil beneath my feet
I inhale my toxic thoughts
exhale the poison that is my heart

Mark Williams

I can't walk wearing tight socks
They keep me from touching
ground, graves and a future
I can't start fires without the scent
of ashes flourishing in my head

Dylan Vallance

I sit here and watch
Every time the train takes off
All the things I want
Always seem to pass me
No hello, no good-bye

Kaleb Stropkovics

Inspiration
A blessing given to our minds
Like snow it can shimmer
But like fire
It can burn

Brittany Johns

I remember
Like it was yesterday
I won't ever forget
The dull light and whispers
The wind swirling around me

Margie Chenetz

Note To Teachers

Dorothy assembled the completed tanka into a class chapbook titled "One Million Things." The frontispiece was a page from *The New Yorker*, turned on its side. Each page contained one tanka and a cutout from a page of text so that shapes (some abstract, some formational) appeared alongside each tanka. Dorothy also contributed a poem, and a list of students' names appeared on the back page. Copies of the chapbook were distributed to all students in the class.

Chapbooks have a long and colourful history in the development of poetic advancement. Mostly assembled by poets promoting their own wares as early as the fifteenth century, chapbooks today come in many varieties. They are simple to put together and serve individual needs as well as collective "promotion" for the arts within the school: education week, library displays, literacy festivals, teaching tools for up-coming classes.

I happily award five stars ***** — the highest possible rating! to teachers, like Dorothy, who join in the writing experience with their students.

The Poetry of Things Before I Could Speak: A Very Short Pedagogical Thought for Teachers Who Juggle Forty Balls in the Air at One Time

Terry Ann Carter

> I've this memory —
>   riding my father's shoulders
>   into the ocean
>   the poetry of things
>   before I could speak

Michael McClintock's award winning tanka has long been a favourite of mine to inspire teens (and their teachers) to begin writing in this "genre." There is something about the universality of this one poem, these simple five lines that strike a chord in every classroom. I have used (borrowed) this tanka hundreds of times, most recently in a class of grade twelve girls, studying "World Literature" with Ms. Annie Jilbert, at United World College of South East Asia, in Singapore. I began by reading the poem in its entirety. Students were asked to jot down the first line and then the fourth and fifth lines. The second and third lines were left "open" for their own memory from early childhood, "the poetry of things, before I could speak." Memories included other visits to the sea, gumboots, a train ride, waving goodbye to a dog. The students were eager to read their poems.

There are many other tanka that might serve in this way: highlight a line or two, then encourage students to fill in the missing lines. "Imitative writing" is a good resource for beginning poets; I encourage students to move to their own poetry as soon as possible.

Part 5: Tanka resources

Websites and magazines

Tankaonline.com is a valuable and informative resource for teaching tanka. Here you will find articles on:

About Tanka and Its History by Amelia Fielden

A Quick Start Guide to Writing Haiku by Jeanne Emrich

Notes of Form, Techniques, and Subject Matter by Michael McClintock

A Tanka Repair Kit by Jeanne Emrich

My Tanka Path by Tom Clausen

Distilling Experience by Margaret Chula

Tanka as Diary by Amelia Fielden

A tanka teachers' guide appears as a public service of the Modern English Tanka Press in cooperation with the Tanka Society of America. http://www.themetpress.com/bookstore/tankateachersguideversion1download.pdf

On this site you will find links to the following tanka magazines (under "Tanka Central")

- *3Lights Gallery*

- *American Tanka*

- *Atlas Poetica (A Journal of Poetry of Place in Contemporary Tanka) **

- *bottle rockets*

- *Eucalypt*

- *Gusts: A Journal of Contemporary Tanka*

- *Lilliput Review*

- *Lynx*

- *Modern English Tanka*

- *Modern Haibun & Tanka Prose*

- *Moonset*

- *Paper Wasp*

- *red lights*

- *Snapshot Press*

- *Ribbons (Tanka Society of America)*

The mission of Tanka Central is to promote the tanka form of poetry; to educate newcomers to tanka about the form's history and future, techniques, and uses, and to work for wider publication of tanka in both specialty and mainstream poetry venues. In order to accomplish this mission, it is our intent to build a megasite that will be the best place to study tanka on the internet, with its own onsite resources, with comprehensive links to other relevant sites, with connections to others who write, read, and publish tanka; it will become the best source for finding places that publish tanka, calls for submissions, etc.

*Atlas Poetica is pleased to announce the long awaited publication of "25 Tanka for Children."

Accompanied by notes for educators, the material is covered by Atlas Poetica Educational Use Policy. The poems range from the humorous to the serious and feature wordplay, whimsy, and insight. Perhaps young for a teenaged reader, yet suggested activities assist the teacher in preparing lesson plans that could be modified for older interests. More information at http://AtlasPoetica.org

A Few Good Books on Tanka

Konkinshu, A Collection of Poems Ancient and Modern, trans. Laurel Rasplica Rodd (Cheng & Tsui, 1996).

Modern Japanese Tanka, by Makoto Ueda (Columbia, 1996).

Footsteps in the Fog, by Michael Dylan Welch (Press Here, 1994).

Tanka Splendor, (AHA, annually to 1999, then online).

Wind Five Folded, ed. Jane and Werner Reichhold (AHA, 1994).

Haiga

Part 1: Definition of haiga

Poetry and paintings on the same page had long been a tradition in China, Japan and Korea. Haiku was painted down the page using a calligraphy brush and sumi-e ink. Haiga is a traditional art form composed of brush painting and calligraphy of haiku poetry. Today, haiga is created with drawings, paintings, photographs and digital technology—marrying image and text so that each is independent of the other, yet producing an artwork mysteriously "new."

Part 2: Examples of traditional haiga

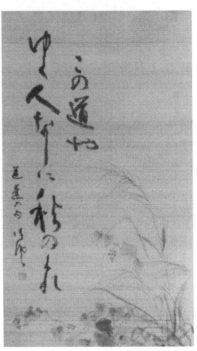

In the words of the artist: "As I work on a traditional Japanese brush painting, I always leave space for the eventual or potential collaboration with a calligrapher (typically we reserve 70% open or white space). The calligrapher's part is to enhance and create harmony between the painted image and the words and concepts conveyed. Sometimes these are a historical haiku by a famous poet, which is transcribed, other times it will be the image that stimulates or generates the idea for an original haiku. Calligraphers on the other hand, work first to create their contribution to the piece, leaving a small space to the artist to enhance the poet's words. The haiku artist, painter and calligrapher are often three different people, working in different sequences, depending on who first begins the process of creating art."

Rebecca Lyn Cragg

Mrs. Yohko Tamaki (haiku poet) spent several months looking at Rebecca's paintings before creating this original haiku. Yohko resides in Wakayama City, where she has been studying haiku with her teacher for over a decade. She is an amateur calligrapher and did the calligraphy in Rebecca's painting, which appears in the left panel on the previous page. The English translation appears below:

> ripples of the waves,
> lamentation of the light
> in the fall sunshine

Kiyoko Ogawa was the calligrapher/painter for the textile piece, which appears on the right. She carried out an international exchange through calligraphy in Brisbane, Australia in 1999, in Whangarey, New Zealand in 2001, and in Ulan Bator, Mongolia in 2002. In 2003, Kiyoko was awarded the prestigious Miyazaki Daily Newspaper Award for her outstanding and vigorous efforts in regard to international cultural exchange efforts. The translation of Bashō's haiku, by Rebecca Lyn Cragg, follows:

> On this deserted path,
> Not a person in sight,
> Autumn evening comes.

Part 3: Examples of contemporary haiga

in a frozen world
it's hard to imagine
spring

In the words of the poet, Naia, who created both the haiga appearing on this page and the next: "When creating haiga, I almost always begin with the image. I paint with watercolors, generally in a cross between impressionist and abstract styles. Often the outcome of a painting session surprises me because I typically don't begin painting with a subject or outcome in mind. I start with brush strokes and color combinations, until a particular combination begins to take on its own shape. Sometimes this happens quickly, and other times it may take several hours. Once a painting is finished, I sit with the image and study it intensely until associations begin forming. From those associations a haiku eventually emerges that adds a deeper, richer, fuller dimension to the image. Haiku and painting are then combined to create the synergistic expression called haiga."

rising above it . . .
summer
in the humming city

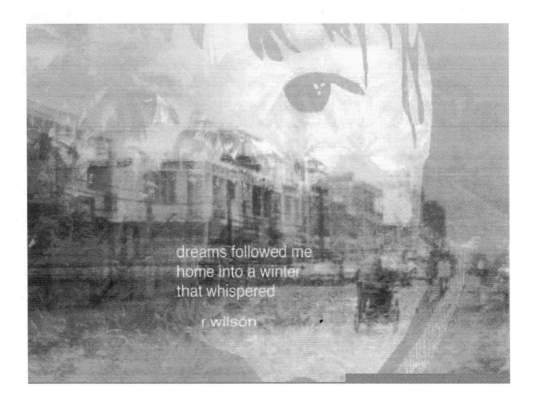

This example of contemporary haiga by robert d. wilson employs layers of photographs and embedded text.

This example of contemporary haiga is by Pamela Miller Ness, featuring embroidered image and haiku on linen.

Part 4: Images for inspiration

The images that appear in this section can be used by students to inspire haiku so that they can fashion their own haiga. Students may also create their own photographs, line drawings, or images of other kinds.

Photographs

Paul Benoit

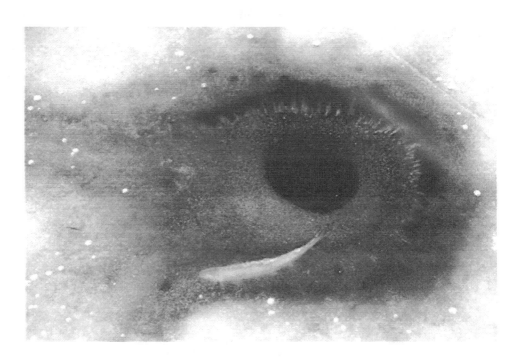

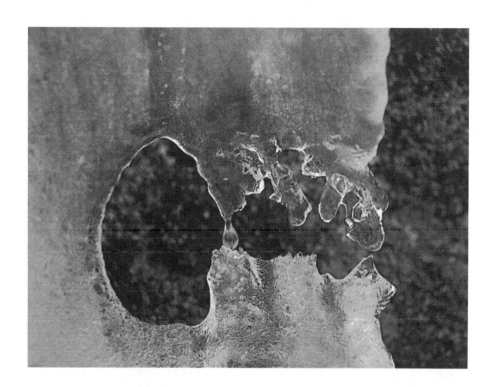

These photos were taken by Paul Benoit with a Nikon D 80, and were tweaked as needed with iPhoto on a Mac. Some photos are the equivalent of "point and shoot" opportunities, but the ones he values most represent a special effort to find.

Line Drawings

Matt Cipov

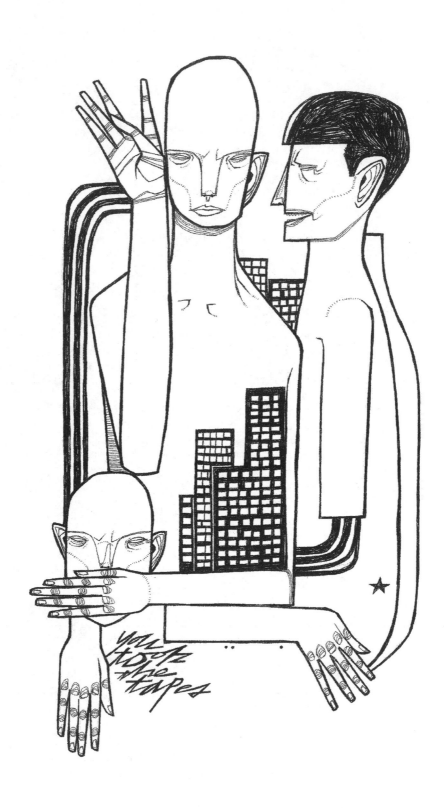

Part 5: Article of inspiration for teachers and students

Jim Kacian's article "Haiga: Pictures and Words Together at Last" is a review of poetry and image used in advertising, revolutionary posters, surreal art, and Japanese traditional haiga. He invites us to enrich ourselves with past examples of art to inspire modern day haiga.

Haiga: Pictures and Words Together at Last

Jim Kacian

People have been putting text to pictures practically from the time writing was invented. In fact, the first writing was pictures. Today we see photos with captions in newspapers and on the web, read graphic novels and comic books, are inundated by advertising and graffiti, and hang posters on our walls. It might be surprising to learn, then, that this collaboration of word and image is actually quite rare in "high art," the world of museums and commissions.

Given that the visual and the verbal are the two most powerful and frequently employed elements of communications, it might seem odd that they have not often shared space in the artistic mind. But it is for the very reason of their power that they do not, since each medium is so demanding of attention in its own right, an overlap between them often a distracts from the other. A painting is usually "about" itself, and not about some words

used to describe it. In fact, words can be considered an intrusion on the artistic space which the painting commands. Think about this a moment: imagine a famous painting, let's say Van Gogh's *Starry Night*. We can easily conjure up the image, and consider it simply as an image. Now imagine the same image, but with words below, or worse, in the midst of, the painting.

Our relationship with the image is changed, because the words shift our attention from our contemplation of the image to finding some relationship between the image and these words. We know this because this image has been used for advertising purposes, and so has lost some of its power to excite the imagination purely as image.

So it's no small task to bring image and text together and not have them disrupt one another. An even larger challenge would be to make them actually work together so that if you removed either element, something would be lost. In an ad using *Starry Night* we could easily get rid of the words and feel that the image was just fine as it was. What if we could add words in some way to it so that it actually made it better? Is this even possible?

This is the task which haiga has set for itself. Haiga is a combination of image and text where the two elements support one another. In order to succeed at this, some special circumstances must be present. That's what this short paper is going to explore.

Probably the most common pairing of word and image in current use is the poster. You probably have many on your walls at home. When you look at them, what do you look at first? Do you look at the picture, or do you read the words? Or have the words become another part of the picture, a visual element that might also be read, but needn't be for the poster to work? Most people, after a time, stop reading their posters and identify the whole thing as one large image made up of many small elements, including words. This is because we are a visual species (unlike, say, bats or bears). We are most stimulated by what our eyes see, even if they are not as sharp as those of, say, eagles.

Posters have been around for a long time. Look at this one, from the Russian Revolution by an unknown artist in 1919. You don't need to read cyrilic characters to get a sense of what the poster is saying: the power and orderliness of the text is underscored by the horses, symbols of domesticated power, brought up to the mark by their human riders. "Mount your Horses, Workers and Peasants!" the poster exhorts, and the unity of the "goal" is seen to be compelling enough to unite horses and even men of decidedly different breeds and ethnic origins. A powerful message in a brief compass.

Perhaps the second most common combination of image and test is calligraphy. Calligraphy is writing that uses the shapes of the letters or whole words to suggest an image. There is a famous example by the French poet Apollinaire entitled "Il pleut." This poem "illustrates" its subject by imitating it because the words fall down the page, just like rain. Not all calligraphy is as obvious as this, but this is its basic strategy. A few well-known paintings have used words directly as objects within the paintings. One of the most famous of these is this painting by Rene Magritte of two pipes.

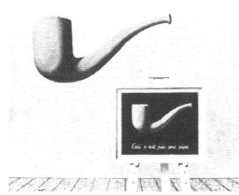

The lower pipe seems to be on a kind of chalkboard above the "hand-written" words "Ceci n'est pas une pipe" —"This is not a pipe." Magritte was a member of an art movement called Dada, which sought to create new inspiration by calling into question all the normal perceptions of living, including the way we casually blend the verbal with the visual. Most people, when asked what they were looking at in this painting, would answer "a pipe." Magritte brings to the surface the easy mistake we make in taking the one for the other, an image of something for the real thing.

These have largely been the strategies Western artists have used to try to combine word and image, and they work fine, even if they are limited in what they accomplish. What if, however, we didn't want to advocate a position (as the poster does), or turn a piece of writing into its own illustration (as the calligraphy does) or make a philosophical point (as the painting does)? What if we wanted to stimulate some other effect in our audience? How might we do it?

Some artists who lived in feudal Japan pondered this very question. These artists possessed two distinct skills —they could paint, mostly in ink washes in the style of the day; and they could write poetry, often haiku. Was it possible to combine their skills in a pleasing artistic whole?

We know the problem they were going to encounter: how do you keep one element from dominating the other? The solution they discovered was a very interesting one, and not one that is immediately obvious. What they decided to do was to create both paintings and poems that did not attempt to say everything about the subject at hand, but rather merely hinted at one aspect. This was a subtle way of involving the reader or observer in the

process of creating the whole artistic event. And when they came to combine the words with the image, often they would choose elements that just barely referred to each other, what we might call a tangential interest, which made the person trying to make sense of the work of art imagine an even larger context where both elements might fit. The observer as the missing element in the work of art is perhaps the greatest contribution eastern art brought to general culture. The art form that was thus created is called haiga (*haikai* painting).

Let's look at some examples. This first, by the artist/poet Oshima Ryota (1718–1787), is extremely subtle. If we simply look at it as a picture, what we see is most of a charcoal brazier, with the calligraphy of the words suggesting smoke rising. We might expect a poem about fire or smoke, or the cold night. Instead the poem reads:

> looking at the light
> there is a wind
> this night of snow

How beautiful it is to watch the free flight of descending snowflakes—if we're comfortably warm. The basket is casually sketched, and to echo its peripheral status in the poem actually falls off the edge of the paper. The hint of wind is caught in the calligraphy, with its sinuous curves and wide vertical spacings. The visual is subordinated to the verbal in this work, but in such a beguiling fashion, and so modestly, that it is easily assimilated into the world of the poem, and in fact infinitely deepens it.

This is what haiga can do at its best—bring disparate elements together so that their two worlds deepen each other. It is very difficult to do, but when done well, aspires to the highest realm of art.

Another strategy the early Japanese practitioners of haiga used was the poem/portrait. This kind of work depends on the viewer already knowing quite a lot about the history of haiku and haiga, since the portraits were of famous poets who had created earlier haiga. The master of this style was Yosa Buson (1716–1783), who was also one of the great haiku poets in the

history of haiku. In this haiga he honors his predecessor Bashō, another of the great haiku masters. The poems reads:

> when speaking
> the lips turn cold —
> autumn wind

This is not one of the most famous or revered of Bashō's poems, but is greatly enhanced by this cleverly planned and powerfully rendered portrait. Bashō appears far older here than in any other portraits of him (he died at age fifty-one), the strategy being to portray wisdom through agedness. Buson is claiming a spiritual kinship with Bashō, and honoring him by painting him wiser (that is, older) than he in fact was. Notice too how his figure, though dead now for over a hundred years, flows out to more than fill the space. His presence remains overwhelming to the painter even after all these years. The traveling clothes also suggest Bashō's common humanity. And, as the self-proclaimed direct descendant, spiritually, of Bashō, Buson claims all these powers for himself as well.

This is not a casual sketch, jotted quickly. This is from the tradition of high art, with calculated effects and sure technique. It functions in the way that mainstream art usually functions, by appropriating the symbols of power recognized in the technique and exploiting them.

Compare this to the much more modest self-portrait by another of the great haiku masters, Kobayashi Issa (1763–1827). Issa was nowhere near the artist that Buson was, and he wisely limited himself to sketches, often making fun of himself as a country rube and hack artist and belittling the way he makes creatures look in his paintings. What do you think he might be saying about himself in this haiga? (Answer next page.)

This seemingly diffident portrait, comical in aspect, surprises us with its heartfelt and mordant poem:

> A world of grief and pain,
> Even when cherry-blossoms
> Have bloomed.

Even at the most wonderful time of year, at the peak of spring under a canopy of the most beautiful blossoms, we are reminded that all life is suffering, says the poet. Who could have guessed from that sly sketch the pain the poet felt? And to the poem the poet added the words "The people, and Issa, too," taking in all humanity, omitting no one, in the sweep of his little poem.

Haiga was one of Japanese culture's highest attainments in its heyday, in the middle of the nineteenth century, but as it is an extremely difficult art, requiring mastery of two artistic pursuits, poetry and painting, it could not sustain its pre-eminence, and fell into disuse by the beginning of the twentieth century. It has had something of a small renaissance in the past 50 years, both in Japan and around the world, spurred in part by new cultures coming to appreciate the way and world that haiku offers in its small compass. So how do contemporary poets create haiga? How is it different from the art of two centuries ago?

One strategy, of course, is to pay homage to the artist/poets of the past by creating work "in the manner of." That's what Jeanne Emrich strives for in much of her work, such as the work seen here.

Though the world is very different in many ways, some things have not changed across the years and in different cultures — we are still awed by the actions of natural forces in our everyday world. Here the piling up of snow on a ladder, a common-place, may seem the most beautiful thing in

winter moon …
undisturbed snow
on the cabin steps

the world, a gift from nature to ourselves, no matter the culture or era.

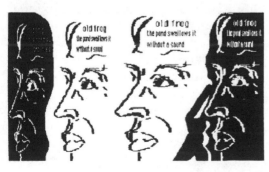

With new media and new inspiration to draw upon, it's not surprising that haiga today looks quite a bit different. However, the best work still maintains a tangential and sketch-like relationship between the elements of the work. Look at what David Gershator has made of the poem/portrait tradition in this piece which evokes the early days of computer graphics and impact printers.

He calls upon the same poet whom Buson portrayed, Bashō, but his version is multiple and less grand, ambiguous. Is that one of Bashō's great poems on his "mind"? And it seems to have staying power, remaining on his mind in each of several iterations. It is useful to recall that Bashō urged his disciples to turn their poems over and over in their minds to polish them before letting them see the light of day, and this would seem to be exactly what the poet himself is doing in this instance.

the first snowfall . . .
searching for something I know
I'll never find

Compare this with Zario Zolo's interesting non-portrait haiga, subtly tangential in the same fashion as the Ryoha piece we looked at first.

The visual element of this suggests a woods looming up in the distance, seemingly out of nowhere, but directly in our path. The density of the wash of foliage makes it appear impassable, while the strong verticals give it a solidity as well. But upon closer inspection, perhaps this isn't woods at all, but something nearer, perhaps an extreme close-up view of the hairs on our body. Most likely we are in the interior spaces of the artist's mind, and this is some figurative version of hell, a hell where the only certainty is that of frustration. And so the poem proves the point: finding anything in this morass will be a truly trying experience. In any event, the poet already knows the result of his search, and all he finds in the end is—art.

There is one more technique, unavailable in Buson's day, that is very popular with contemporary poets who are trying their hands at haiga, and that is the pairing of haiku with photographs. By definition this is going to be a very difficult challenge, since a photograph, taken directly from "reality," will not often lend itself to an ambiguous, open reading, and so will most likely dominate the ensemble effect. This is a great challenge to the artist, and while most attempts so far haven't been very successful, there is no reason not to try. Haiga using photographs has only just begun to be explored, and awaits its avatar. Perhaps you will be the one who discovers how to make them work together, and so become one of the great innovators in this ancient art. Good luck!

Part 5: Haiga resources

Before you compose your own haiga, it is important to view some haiga examples. You can find thousands of haiga online, both traditional and contemporary. An online gallery of haiga or haiku painting appears at http://www.reedscontemporaryhaiga.com. Here you will find the best of haiga, articles, and interviews from past years of the companion annual hard copy anthology, as well as new work by leading haiga artists. This site includes:

• *The Turning Point—a haiga exhibition by Raffael de Gruttola and Peggy McClure*

• *Starlit Mountain: How White Space and Imagination Work in Haiga—an interview with Jeanne Emrich*

• *The Touch of Hand and Brush—an interview with Stephen Addiss*

• *Still Surprising—haiga by Stephen Addiss*

• *Every Time—haiga by Susan Frame and others*

• *The Art of Sumi-e Painting—an interview with Susan Frame*

• *Hide and Seek—haiga by Gary LeBel*

• *Haiga and the Art of Digital Rendering—an interview with Kuniharu Shimizu by Jeanne Emrich*

• *The Spirit of Haiga—an interview with Ion Codrescu by Jeanne Emrich and also articles on the "history of haiga" and "how to write haiku."*

Another source is http://www.haigaonline.com which includes examples of traditional haiga, experimental haiga, contemporary haiga, and haiga workshops.

Haiga: Japanese art and poetry is a website maintained by Ray Rasmussen and the World Haiku Club whose members contribute haiku poetry and images for the haiga compositions. The entry page is a digital modification of the Great Wave of Kanagawa. It comes from a series of Thirty-six Views of Mount Fuji, Edo period (1615–1831) by Katsushika Hokusai, and is part of the H. O. Havemeyer Collection at the Metropolitan Museum of Arts. The digital image was made from a scan of the print of the image.

http://www.dailyhaiga.org, an edited journal of contemporary and conditional haiga. Editors: Linda M. Pilarski (Associate Editor), Patrick M. Pilarski (Poetry Editor), Nicole Pakan (Art Work).

Contributors

Roberta Beary was born and raised in New York City and lived in Tokyo for five years of haiku study. Her individual poems, an unconventional hybrid of haiku and senryu, have been honored throughout North America, Europe and Asia for their innovative style. Her book of short poems, *The Unworn Necklace* (1st Hardcover edition 2011), selected as a William Carlos Williams Book Award finalist (Poetry Society of America), was named a Haiku Society of America Merit Book Award prize winner. More information about Roberta Beary's poetry can be found on her website http://www.robertabeary.com.

Dr. Paul Benoit has practiced Plastic Surgery in Ottawa since 1974. Almost all of his photos are from Heney Lake in the Upper Gatineau Valley north of Ottawa, with many from the Gatineau Park. He delights in finding the images as he explores new trails, or rediscovers different features in familiar areas as the seasons change.

An international prize-winning haiku poet and book artist, **Rick Black** is the founder of Turtle Light Press—a small press dedicated to handcrafted books, fine art cards and photography. He studied Hebrew literature at The Hebrew University in Jerusalem on a post-graduate scholarship and subsequently joined the Jerusalem bureau of *The New York Times*. Learn more about Rick and the press at http://www.turtlelightpress.com.

John Brandi's latest book, *Seeding the Cosmos*, presents selections from 30 years of his haiku practice. In 2009 he gave the keynote speech for the Haiku North America Conference in Ottawa, Canada. In 2010 he was invited to India for the release of *Blue Sky Ringing*, a trilingual book of his haiku. He lives in New Mexico where he teaches through the Witter Bynner Foundation for Poetry.

Dr. Randy M. Brooks is the Dean of the College of Arts & Sciences and Professor of English at Millikin University. He teaches courses on the global haiku tradition at Millikin with student work available on the MU Haiku website: http://old.millikin.edu/haiku. He and his wife, Shirley Brooks, are co-editors and publishers of Brooks Books, and edit *Mayfly* haiku magazine. He has served as web editor of Modern Haiku magazine and serves on the Executive Committee of the Haiku Society of America as Electronic Media Officer, editing the *Frogpond* web sampler and maintaining the society website.

Matt M. Cipov lives for the love of art. Some people live to make joyful noise, other people live to write joyful words. Matt has the need to make joyful lines. He draws and draws and draws. Take away his time for art, he'll be a sad boy indeed (http://www.mattcipov.com).

Rebecca Lyn Cragg, founder and president of Camellia Teas of Ottawa studied Suibokuga (ink painting) in Japan from 1998–2005. During that time she focused on landscape painting with her teacher, Mr. Hiroshi Tamaki. Rebecca currently teaches traditional Japanese Brush painting, the Way of Tea, Ikebana and Kimono dressing at her studio in Ottawa, Ontario. See her website at http://www.camelliateas.net.

John J. Dunphy is a prolific author of prose and poetry. His chapbooks include *Old Soldiers Fading Away* (Pudding House, 2006); *Stellar Possibilities* (Sam's Dot Publishing, 2006); and *Zen Koanhead* (Second Reading Publications, 2008). His non-fiction works published by the History Press are *From Christmas to Twelfth Night in Southern Illinois* (2010) and *Abolitionism and the Civil War in Southwestern Illinois* (2011). He owns The Second Reading Book Shop in Alton, Illinois, which he runs with the assistance of several on-site felines.

Amelia Fielden is an Australian. She is a professional translator of Japanese literature, and an enthusiastic writer of tanka in English. To date Amelia has translated, or co-translated, 15 collections of contemporary Japanese tanka. In 2007 Amelia and co-translator, Kozue Uzawa, were awarded the Donald Keene Prize for Translation of Japanese Literature by Columbia University, New York, for their anthology *Ferris Wheel, 101 Modern and Contemporary Japanese Tanka* (Cheng & Tsui, Boston, 2006). Six volumes of Amelia's own poetry have also been published.

Garry Gay was born in Glendale, California, in 1951, and has been a professional photographer for the past 37 years. He started writing haiku in 1975. In 1989 he co-founded the Haiku Poets of Northern California and became their first president (1989-90)and was elected again (2001-2009). In 1991 he founded Haiku North America, a biennial haiku conference and in 1996 he co-founded the American Haiku Archives in Sacramento, California. He is the creator of the poetic form called Rengay and the author of *The Billboard Cowboy, The Silent Garden, Wings of Moonlight, River Stones, Along the Way,* and *The Unlocked Gate* published with John Thompson.

LeRoy Gorman has taught high school English for over thirty years and has been trying to write haiku for just as long. A few of his books include: *heart's garden* (Guernica), *whose smile the ripple warps* (Underwhich), *wind in the keys* (High Coo Press), *parallel journey/voyage parallèle* (with André Duhaime, Éditions Asticou), *glass bell* (King's Road Press), *where sky meets* sky (Nietzsche's Brolly), *flurries* (Timberline), *nothing personal* (Proof Press). He is Editor of *Haiku Canada Review* and Life Member of Haiku Canada.

Penny Harter's work appears in numerous journals and anthologies. Among her many books, six feature haiku and related genres. Recent books include *Recycling Starlight* (2010), *The Beastie Book* (2009), *The Night Marsh* (2008), and *Buried in the Sky* (2002). A featured reader at the 2010 Dodge Poetry Festival, Harter has received three poetry fellowships from the New Jersey State Council on the Arts, the Mary Carolyn Davies Award from the Poetry Society of America, the William O. Douglas Nature Writing Award, and a fellowship from VCCA for January, 2011. As a visiting poet-in-residence for the NJSCA, she leads workshops for students of all ages, as well as faculty.

Jim Kacian is founder and director of The Haiku Foundation, owner of Red Moon Press, author of 20 books of haiku and editor of scores more. His own haiga have been exhibited on five continents.

Deborah P Kolodji is the president of the Science Fiction Poetry Association and the moderator of the Southern California Haiku Study Group. Her work has appeared in *Frogpond, bottle rockets, Modern Haiku, the Heron's Nest, Strange Horizons, Star*Line, Haiku Canada Review, poeticdiversity, Chicken Soup for the Dieter's Soul, THEMA*, and many other places. When she's not writing haiku, she can be found hiking to waterfalls and wandering the beaches of Southern California.

Dorothy Mahoney is an English teacher and Instructional Coach at Essex District High School, Windsor, Ontario. She has two books of poetry with Black Moss Press and is included in two anthologies by Cranberry Tree Press.

Michael McClintock has been a poet, editor and critic in the short form genres of haiku, tanka, and senryu since the 1960s, and has served as contributing editor to *Modern English Tanka* (2006-2009) and president of the Tanka Society of America (2004-2010). Recent works include *Meals at Midnight* (Modern English Tanka Press, 2008), *Sketches from the San Joaquin* (Turtle Light Press, 2009), and the anthology *Streetlights: Poetry of Urban Life in Modern English Tanka* (Modern English Tanka Press, 2009). He currently writes the uniquely interactive column "Tanka Café" for *Ribbons: Tanka Society of America Journal* and makes his home in Clovis, California.

A native of Northern-Ontario, **Mike Montreuil** lives in Ottawa, Ontario with his family and a trio of cats. His Japanese form poems, in English and in French, have been published in various print and on-line journals throughout the world. He has published *An Armor All Shine Tan Renga* with Claudia Coutu Radmore, *wet cement: the cradle 2 haiku anthology* (editor, 2010), and *The Neighbours Are Talking, Haibun*, (2011). When he is not watching hockey, Mike can be found in one of the many coffee shops in Ottawa.

Naia is a fifth generation native Californian. She attended college at California State Polytechnic University (Cal Poly) in San Luis Obispo. Naia's poetry and haiga have appeared in books, anthologies, e-journals, newsletters, and magazines in the U.S. and internationally. She belongs to a number of haiku and tanka poetry associations and currently serves as Haiku Society of America Regional Coordinator for California. Some of her published work is posted at http://www.naia.ws.

Pamela Miller Ness has been writing haiku and tanka for the past 15 years, has published her poetry in a variety of international journals, been featured in the *Red Moon Anthology* and anthologized in *A New Resonance II*, and has published six chapbooks. She has served as President, Vice-President, and newsletter editor of the Haiku Society of America. She chaired the organizing committee for Haiku North America 2003 in New York City. Pamela's awards include first prize in the San Francisco / HPNC International Tanka Contest, the Tanka Society of America International Tanka Contest, and winner and finalist in the Snapshot Haiku Calendar contest and the TWA Penumbra Haiku Contest.

Editor of the annual Haiku Canada Anthology, **Claudia Coutu Radmore** is the President of Kado Ottawa, a Japanese-form writers' group in Ottawa, Ontario. She helps select tanka for *Gusts,* Canada's Tanka Society magazine and has published lyric as well as haiku, tanka and renga internationally. She is a member of Haiku Canada, The Haiku Society of America, and Haiku North America, and has helped organize Haiku Canada Weekends and the Haiku North America Conference in Ottawa. Her bilingual book of tanka, *Your Hands Discover me/ Tes mains me découvrent* (2010) was published by *Éditions du tanka francophone*, Montréal.

Grant Savage is an Ottawa poet and photographer who began writing haiku in 1986. His haiku, tanka, and senryu have appeared in anthologies and journals in North America and Japan. In 1994, he and Ruby Spriggs published a book of renku *The Swan's Wings*. He won first place in the Drevniok Award Contest (1999), and published *Their White With Them* with Bondi Studios (2006).

Dr. Richard Schnell, State University of New York Distinguished Service Professor of Counseling, Jungian psychotherapist, and former mental health & drug treatment clinic treatment director, fell in love with Chinese poetry in Santa Fe in 1998, and later Japanese haiku. Author of *Adirondack Haiku: Kayaking through Fog* (2004), his haiku and renku have been published in Romania, Ireland, Canada and the US. His haiku are typically visual, and his senryu self-deprecating. Schnell organized the International Haiku Festival 2008 on Lake Champlain. A member of Haiku Canada and Haiku North America, he teaches Honors Program courses on *Haiku & Healing*.

Jessica Tremblay was born in Chicoutimi (Québec) in 1973. Her haiku were featured in the Montréal métro (La poésie prend le métro 2007), posted in the Vancouver buses and skytrains (Vancouver Cherry Blossom Festival Haiku Invitational 2008 — Best BC poem) and sculpted in a stone at the VanDusen botanical garden. She won 2 awards from Japan (Mainichi, 2007; Kusamakura, 2009). She lives in Vancouver BC where she creates a weekly haiku comic called Old Pond (http://oldpond.voila.net).

Cor van den Heuvel has been writing haiku since he first learned about it in San Francisco in 1958. Best known as the editor of three editions of *The Haiku Anthology* and *Baseball Haiku*, he has also published ten chapbooks of his own haiku. He has won three Merit Book awards from the Haiku Society of America and in 2002 he received the Masaoka Shiki International Haiku Prize in Matsuyama. His latest book is *A Boy's Seasons: Haibun Memoirs*, published by Single Island Press.

Michael Dylan Welch is the vice president of the Haiku Society of America, cofounder of the Haiku North America conference and the American Haiku Archives, and founder and first president of the Tanka Society of America. He has published thousands of his haiku and has won or judged many haiku contests. He has been involved with the Vancouver Cherry Blossom Festival's Haiku Invitational since its inception in 2006, serving as a judge each year except 2009. His website can be found at http://www.graceguts.com.

robert d. wilson is co-publisher & co-owner of *Simply Haiku*. He's the author of *Jack Fruit Moon*, *Vietnam Ruminations*, and a murder mystery novel, *Late for Mass*, a columnist for *Teacher Librarian Magazine*, the director of a community day school, and a poet. He lives in the Philippines and California, near Yosemite National Park.

Jeffrey Winke is the co-editor of the first small press North American haiku anthology, the *Third Coast Haiku Anthology*, which was published in 1977. He is the former associate editor of Modern Haiku magazine, considered by Tokyo's Museum of Haiku to be the best English-language haiku journal. Jeffrey has been writing haiku for almost 40 years. His most recent book, *What's Not There: Selected Haiku of Jeffrey Winke* is a 2002 Merit Book Award winner. His motion graphics haiku collection called Chances can be viewed at http//www.bytestudios.com/winke and has been designated a "Cool Website." Jeff's haibun have been published extensively and a collection of haibun entitled *I'll Tell You So*, was published by Cross+Roads Press. He lives and works in Milwaukee, Wisconsin.

Sherry Zhou is a young poet. At the time of writing, she was in Grade 8 at Crofton House School in Vancouver, British Columbia. She devours novels every day and loves sketching, painting, and working with clay. Sherry is a very passionate poet and also devotes herself to playing sports. As well, she enjoys harmonizing on the piano and learning new things. Sherry's favourite inspirations are the ocean and cherry blossoms; she is a committed member of Haiku Canada and Pacific-kana. She lives with her parents, her plethora of fish, and three turtles in Vancouver.

A thank you to the following poets who answered my Call for Submissions and who offered words of encouragement throughout the project. Their work appears with permission: Marco Fraticelli (haiku), George Swede (haiku), Michael McClintock (haiku and tanka), Emiko Miyashita (haiku), Philomene Kocher, (haiku and tanka), Michael Dylan Welch (haiku), Pearl Pirie (haiku), John Stevenson (haiku), Francine Banwarth (haiku), Ce Rosenow (haiku), Angela Leuck (haiku and tanka), Dorothy Howard (haiku), Stanford M. Forrester (haiku), Penny Harter (haiku), Lenard D. Moore (haiku), Lois Harvey (tanka), Tom Clausen (tanka), Owen Bullock (tanka), Pamela Babusci (tanka), Barry George (tanka), Helen Buckingham (tanka), Guy Simser (tanka), and Carole MacRury (tanka), Lenard D. Moore and Fay Aoyagi (renga), Richard Straw (rengay).

Works Cited

Bashō, M. (1980). *A haiku journey: Bashō's narrow road to a far province.* Translated by Dorothy Britton. Tokyo, Japan: Kodansha International.

Brandi, J. (2006). *Water shining beyond the fields.* New Mexico: Tres Chicas Books.

Dewey, J. (1915). *Schools for tomorrow.* New York: E. P. Dutton.

Eisner, E. W. (2002). *The arts and the creation of mind.* Harrisonburg, VA: R. R. Donnelly & Sons.

Forster, E. M. (1984). *A passage to India.* San Diego: Harcourt Brace & Co.

Gaylie, V. (2008). The Poetry Garden: Ecoliteracy in an Urban School. *Language & Literacy, 10*(2).

Harter, P. (1987). *The monkey's face.* Fanwood, NJ: From Here Press.

Higginson, W. J., & Harter, P. (1985, 2009). *The haiku handbook: How to write, teach, and appreciate haiku.* New York: Kodansha International.

Kocher, P. (2009). Inviting Connection Through the Gap in Haiku. *Language & Literacy: A Canadian Educational E-Journal, 11*(1).

MacRury, C. (2008). *In the company of crows: Haiku and tanka between the tides.* Eldersburg, MD: Black Cat Press.

Ontario Ministry of Education. (2009). *Acting Today, Shaping Tomorrow: A Policy Framework for Environmental Education in Ontario Schools.*

Rosenow, C. (2010). *Pacific.* Livermore, CA: Mountain Gate Press.

Savage, G. (2006). *Their white with them.* Carlton Place, ON: Bondi Studios.

Shakespeare, W. (1992). *The tragedy of Hamlet.* New York: Washington Square Press.

Swede, G. (2002). The Haiku in Canada: The Formative Years, 1965-1985. *Haiku Canada Newsletter, XVI*(1), 8-13.

van den Heuvel, C. (2010). *A Boy's Seasons: Haibun Memoirs.* Portsmouth, NH: Single Island Press.

Yoshino, Y. (2000). *budding sakura: haiku of Yoshiko Yoshino*. (J. Stamm, Trans.). Evanston, IL: Deep North Press.

Yoshino, Y. (2001). *Tsuru*. (L. Gurga & E. Miyashita, Trans.). Evanston, IL: Deep North Press.

Made in the USA
Charleston, SC
15 June 2011